new interchange

English for international communication

Jack C. Richards

with Jonathan Hull and Susan Proctor

workbook

2

New Interchange Workbook
revision prepared by Jonathan Hull.

CAMBRIDGE
UNIVERSITY PRESS

PUBLISHED BY THE PRESS SYNDICATE OF THE UNIVERSITY OF CAMBRIDGE
The Pitt Building, Trumpington Street, Cambridge, United Kingdom

CAMBRIDGE UNIVERSITY PRESS
The Edinburgh Building, Cambridge CB2 2RU, UK
40 West 20th Street, New York, NY 10011–4211, USA
477 Williamstown Road, Port Melbourne, VIC 3207, Australia
Ruiz de Alarcón 13, 28014 Madrid, Spain
Dock House, The Waterfront, Cape Town 8001, South Africa

http://www.cambridge.org

First published 1998
19th printing 2003

New Interchange Workbook 2 has been developed from *Interchange* Workbook 2,
first published by Cambridge University Press in 1991.

Printed in Hong Kong, China

Typeface New Century Schoolbook   *System* QuarkXPress®   [AH]

A catalog record for this book is available from the British Library

ISBN 0 521 62862 8 Student's Book 2
ISBN 0 521 62861 X Student's Book 2A
ISBN 0 521 62860 1 Student's Book 2B
ISBN 0 521 62859 8 Workbook 2
ISBN 0 521 62858 X Workbook 2A
ISBN 0 521 62857 1 Workbook 2B
ISBN 0 521 62856 3 Teacher's Edition 2
ISBN 0 521 62855 5 Teacher's Manual 2
ISBN 0 521 62854 7 Class Audio Cassettes 2
ISBN 0 521 62852 0 Student's Audio Cassette 2A
ISBN 0 521 62652 8 Student's Audio Cassette 2B
ISBN 0 521 62853 9 Class Audio CDs 2
ISBN 0 521 62851 2 Student's Audio CD 2A
ISBN 0 521 62850 4 Student's Audio CD 2B
ISBN 0 521 95019 8 Audio Sampler 1–3

Also available
ISBN 0 521 62849 0 Video 2 (NTSC)
ISBN 0 521 62848 2 Video 2 (PAL)
ISBN 0 521 62847 4 Video 2 (SECAM)
ISBN 0 521 62846 6 Video Activity Book 2
ISBN 0 521 62845 8 Video Teacher's Guide 2
ISBN 0 521 63887 9 Video Sampler 1–2
ISBN 0 521 77379 2 Lab Guide 2
ISBN 0 521 77378 4 Lab Cassettes 2
ISBN 0 521 62882 2 New Interchange/Passages
Placement and Evaluation Package
ISBN 0 521 80575 9 Teacher-Training Video with
Video Manual

Book design, art direction, and layout services: Adventure House, NYC
Illustrators: Adventure House, Randy Jones, Susan Ferris Jones, Mark Kaufman, Sam Viviano
Photo researcher: Joan Scafarello

Contents

Acknowledgments *iv*

1 A time to remember *1*

2 Caught in the rush *7*

3 Time for a change! *13*

4 I've never heard of that! *19*

5 Going places *25*

6 Sure. No problem! *31*

7 What's this for? *37*

8 Let's celebrate! *43*

9 Back to the future *49*

10 I don't like working on weekends! *55*

11 It's really worth seeing! *61*

12 It's been a long time! *67*

13 A terrific book, but a terrible movie! *73*

14 So that's what it means! *79*

15 What would you do? *85*

16 What's your excuse? *91*

Acknowledgments

ILLUSTRATORS

Randy Jones 4, 6, 13, 16, 17, 21, 36, 38, 39, 48, 50, 54, 55, 59, 68, 72, 77, 79, 82, 85, 88, 92, 94
Susan Ferris Jones 50
Mark Kaufman 2, 22, 31, 41, 83, 95
Sam Viviano 1, 11, 18, 19, 28, 32, 34, 35, 42, 52, 53, 67, 71, 74, 80, 86, 87, 90, 91

PHOTOGRAPHIC CREDITS

The authors and publishers are grateful for permission to reproduce the following photographs.

3 Photofest

5 © Chuck Savage/The Stock Market

7 (*top row, left to right*) © J. Barry O'Rourke/The Stock Market; © Patricia Schaefer; (*middle row, left to right*) New York City Department of Transportation, Office of Bicycle Programs; © Leverett Bradley/Tony Stone Images; (*bottom row, left to right*) © Jacques Chenet/Woodfin Camp & Associates; © Patricia Schaefer

8 © George Ancona/International Stock Photography

10 (*left to right*) © Dale E. Boyer/Photo Researchers; © Alain Evrard/Gamma Liaison; © Alain Evrard/Gamma Liaison; © Bill Wassman/The Stock Market

12 © Wm. Thawley/courtesy of the Chamber of Commerce of Greater Cape May, New Jersey

14 (*top*) © Gary Moon/Tony Stone Images; (*bottom*) © Randy Masser/International Stock Photography

20 © Roy Morsch/The Stock Market

23 © Steven Needham/Envision

25 © Ronnie Kaufman/The Stock Market

27 (*clockwise from top*) © Bill Bachmann/Leo de Wys; © Tibor Bognár/The Stock Market; © Peter Feibert/Gamma Liaison

29 © Renee Lynn/Tony Stone Images

30 (*left to right*) © John F. Mason/The Stock Market; © Steven Rothfeld/Tony Stone Images

37 (*left to right*) © Bill Bachmann/Photo Researchers; © Jose L. Pelaez/The Stock Market; © Djenidi/Gamma Liaison; © Frank Rosotto/The Stock Market; courtesy of The Sharper Image (1-800-344-4444)

43 (*top*) © Eunice Harris/Photo Researchers; (*bottom*) © Paul Souders/Tony Stone Images

46 (*top*) © David Young Wolff/Tony Stone Images; (*bottom*) © Tom Stewart/The Stock Market

47 (*left to right*) © Benainous-Kurita-Simon/Gamma Liaison; © Bob Thomas/Tony Stone Images; © Gerard Saub/Gamma Liaison; © Porterfield-Chickering/ Photo Researchers

49 © Corbis-Bettmann

51 © A & L Sinibaldi/Tony Stone Images

58 (*top to bottom*) © Paul Barton/The Stock Market; © Ariel Skelley/The Stock Market; © D. Trask/The Stock Market; © James Darell/Tony Stone Images; © Michael Keller/The Stock Market

61 © Bushnell/Soifer/Tony Stone Images

62 (*top row, left to right*) © Alan Smith/Tony Stone Images; © G. Anderson/The Stock Market; © David Ball/The Stock Market; (*bottom row, left to right*) © Alain Evrard/Gamma Liaison; © Jose Fuste Raga/The Stock Market

63 (*top*) © Will & Deni McIntyre/Photo Researchers; (*bottom*) © Tibor Bognár/The Stock Market

64 © Paul Harris/Tony Stone Images

65 © Bill Aron/Tony Stone Images

66 © Hulton Getty Picture Collection/Tony Stone Images

69 © Matthew McVay/Tony Stone Images

70 © Torleif Svensson/The Stock Market

73 Photofest

75 (*both*) Photofest

76 Photofest

78 Photofest

96 © Richard Dunoff/The Stock Market

1 A time to remember

1 Past tense

A Write the past tense of these verbs.

Verb	Past tense	Verb	Past tense
be	was/were	laugh	_____
lose	_____	become	_____
scream	_____	move	_____
get	_____	open	_____
write	_____	have	_____
hide	_____	do	_____

B Complete this paragraph. Use the past tense of each of the verbs in part A.

My best friend in school ___was___ Miguel.
He and I _____ in Mrs. Gilbert's third grade
class, and we _____ friends then.
We often _____ crazy things in class, but I don't
think Mrs. Gilbert ever really _____ mad at us.
For example, Miguel _____ a pet rat named
Curly. Sometimes he _____ it in Mrs. Gilbert's
desk. Later, when she _____ the
drawer, she always _____ loudly
and the class _____ . After two
years, Miguel's family _____ to another town.
We _____ letters to each other for a
few years, but then we _____ contact.
I often wonder what
he's doing now.

1

2 *Complete the questions in this conversation.*

Mary: Are you from around here?

Sílvio: No, I'm from Brazil.

Mary: Oh, really? *Were you born* in Brazil?

Sílvio: No, I wasn't born there, actually. I'm originally from Portugal.

Mary: That's interesting. So, when _____ to Brazil?

Sílvio: I moved to Brazil when I was in elementary school. My parents immigrated there.

Mary: _____ in Brazil?

Sílvio: Yes, I grew up in Brazil.

Mary: Where _____ ?

Sílvio: We lived in Recife. It's a beautiful city in northeast Brazil. Then I went to college.

Mary: _____ to school in Recife?

Sílvio: No, I went to school in São Paolo.

Mary: And when _____ to the United States?

Sílvio: I came here last week. I'm Sílvio Mendes. It's nice to meet you.

Mary: Nice to meet you, too. I'm Mary Burns.

3 *Answer these questions.*

1. Where were you born?

_____

2. Did you grow up there?

_____

3. Did you move when you were a child?

_____

4. When did you begin to learn English?

_____

5. Did you have pets when you were young?

_____

6. What hobbies did you have when you were a kid?

_____

4 *John Travolta*

A Do you know the actor John Travolta? What do you know about him?

B Read about John Travolta.

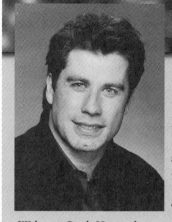

John Travolta

John Travolta was born in 1954 in Englewood, New Jersey. He was the youngest of six children. He wanted to become an actor. In 1975, he played in a TV program called *Welcome Back Kotter* about a high school teacher and his students. The program was very popular and Travolta became famous. Then he started making movies and starred in several successful films. They included *Saturday Night Fever* and *Grease*. Audiences liked his acting and dancing.

In 1977, things suddenly went wrong. His mother and his girlfriend died. Travolta said it was the worst time of his life. He made several unsuccessful films, and thought about giving up as an actor. He is a pilot and has three planes, so he considered becoming a full-time pilot.

But then, when he was working on a movie called *The Experts* in 1987, he met Kelly Preston. The film didn't do well, but John and Kelly fell in love. They got married and they now have a son. They named him Jett because Travolta loves jet planes. Before Jett was born, John and Kelly used to work or go out on weekends, but they prefer to stay home now. The only problem is deciding which home. They have four homes – in California, Florida, Maine, and Hawaii.

In the mid-nineties, John Travolta's luck as an actor changed for the better. He made some very popular films, including *Pulp Fiction*, *Get Shorty*, and *Mad City*. For the second time in his career, he became successful.

C Check (✓) True or False. For statements that are false, write the true information.

	True	False
1. Audiences liked John Travolta in the movie *Saturday Night Fever*.	☐	☐
2. Both his acting and dancing were very popular.	☐	☐
3. All his films have been successful.	☐	☐
4. He worked as a full-time pilot.	☐	☐
5. John and Kelly work or go out on weekends.	☐	☐
6. They have four planes and three homes.	☐	☐

5 **Choose the correct words or phrases.**

1. I used to collect _____*shells*_____ (hobbies/scrapbooks/shells) when
   I was a kid.

2. My favorite pet was a _____ (cat/comic/kid) called Felix.

3. We used to go to _____ (an attic/camp/school) during
   summer vacations. It was really fun.

4. Our neighbors had a great _____ (painting/summer camp/tree house)
   in their backyard. We used to sleep in it.

6 **Look at these childhood pictures of Kate and her brother Peter.**
Complete the sentences using a form of used to.

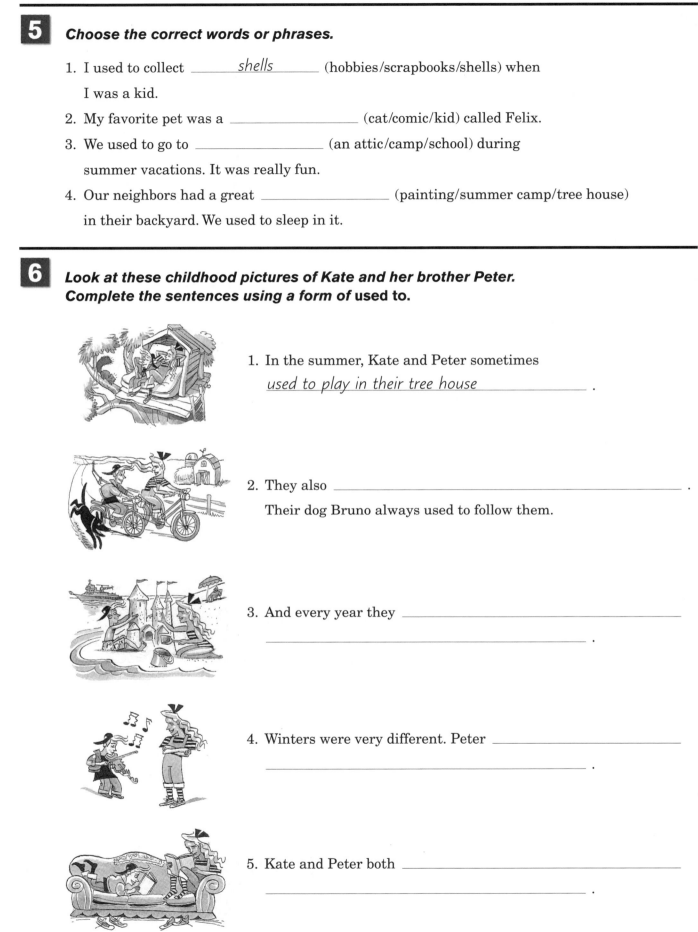

1. In the summer, Kate and Peter sometimes
   used to play in their tree house _____ .

2. They also _____ .
   Their dog Bruno always used to follow them.

3. And every year they _____
   _____ .

4. Winters were very different. Peter _____
   _____ .

5. Kate and Peter both _____
   _____ .

7   *Look at the answers. Write the questions using a form of* used to.

1. A: *What did you use to do in the summer?*
   B: We used to go to the beach.

2. A: _____
   B: No, we didn't collect shells. We used to build sand castles.

3. A: _____
   B: Yes, we did. We used to go swimming for hours. Then we played all kinds of sports.

4. A: Really? What _____
   B: Well, we used to play beach volleyball with some other kids.

5. A: _____
   B: No, we didn't. We used to win!

8   *How have you changed in the last five years? Write answers to these questions.*

1. What hobbies did you use to have five years ago? What hobbies do you have now?

   I used to . . . _____

   Now, . . . _____

2. What kind of music did you use to like then? Who were your favorite singers? What kind of music do you like now?

   _____

   _____

3. What kind of clothes did you use to like to wear? What kind of clothes do you like to wear now?

   _____

   _____

9 *Complete the sentences. Use the past tense of the verbs given.*

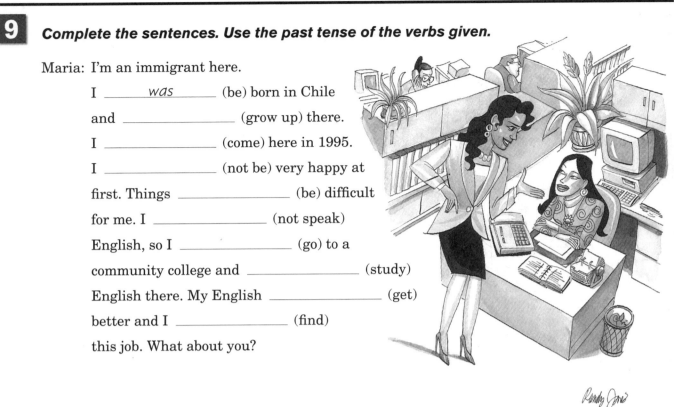

Maria: I'm an immigrant here.

I _____was_____ (be) born in Chile

and _____ (grow up) there.

I _____ (come) here in 1995.

I _____ (not be) very happy at

first. Things _____ (be) difficult

for me. I _____ (not speak)

English, so I _____ (go) to a

community college and _____ (study)

English there. My English _____ (get)

better and I _____ (find)

this job. What about you?

---

10 *Choose the correct responses.*

1. A: Are you from Toronto?

   B: *Well, no. I'm originally from Morocco.*
      - Well, no. I'm originally from Morocco.
      - Neither am I.

2. A: Tell me a little about yourself.

   B: _____
      - Sure. Nice to meet you.
      - What do you want to know?

3. A: How old were you when you moved here?

   B: _____
      - About 16.
      - About 16 years ago.

4. A: Did you learn English here?

   B: _____
      - Yes, I was ten years old.
      - No, I studied it in Morocco.

5. A: By the way, I'm Lisa.

   B: _____
      - What's your name?
      - Glad to meet you.

2 Caught in the rush

1 ***Choose the correct name for each picture.***

☐ bicycle lane	☑ street lights	☐ news stand
☐ bus stop	☐ taxi stand	☐ traffic jam

1. *street lights*

2. _____

3. _____

4. _____

5. _____

6. _____

2 *Problems, problems*

A Choose a solution for each problem.

Problems

1. no places to take children: *build more parks*

2. dark streets: _____

3. no parking spaces: _____

4. crime: _____

5. car accidents: _____

6. traffic jams: _____

> *Solutions*
>
> ☐ install modern street lights
> ☐ build a subway line
> ☐ install more traffic lights
> ☐ hire more police officers
> ☑ build more parks
> ☐ build a public parking garage

B Look at these solutions. Write sentences explaining the problems.
Use *too much, too many,* or *not enough* and the problems in part A.

1. *There aren't enough places to take children.*
   The city should build more parks.

2. _____
   The city should hire more police officers.

3. _____
   The city should install modern street lights.

4. _____
   The city should build a subway line.

5. _____
   The city should install more traffic lights.

6. _____
   The city should build a public parking garage.

C Find another way to say the problems in part B. Begin each
sentence with *There should be more/less/fewer . . . .*

1. *There should be more places to take children.*

2. _____
   _____

3. _____
   _____

4. _____
   _____

5. _____
   _____

6. _____
   _____

3 *City blues*

A Match the words in columns A and B. Write the compound nouns.

A	B	
☑ subway	☑ district	1. <u>subway lines</u>
☑ business	☑ lines	2. <u>AIR POLLUTION.</u>
☑ parking	☐ system	3. <u>POLICE OFFICERS.</u>
☑ air	☑ officers	4. <u>PARKING GARAGES.</u>
☑ police	☑ pollution	5. <u>BUSINESS DISTRICT</u>
☐ train	☑ garages	6. <u>TRAIN SYSTEM.</u>

B Complete this letter to a newspaper, using the compound nouns in part A.

Dear Editor,

Life in this city needs to be improved. For one thing, there are too many cars, and there is too much smog, especially at rush hour. The <u>air pollution</u> is terrible. This problem is particularly bad downtown in the <u>BUSINESS DISTRICT</u>. Too many people drive their cars to work.

So what should we do about it? I think there should be more <u>POLICE OFFICERS</u> at busy intersections. They could stop traffic jams. We also need fewer <u>PARKING GARAGE</u> downtown. The city spends too much money building them. It's easy to park, so too many people drive to work. On the other hand, the city doesn't spend enough on public transportation. There aren't enough <u>SUBWAY LINES</u>, and the <u>TRAIN SYSTEM.</u> needs a lot of improvement.

C Write about a problem in a city you know. Write about the problem in the first paragraph. Suggest solutions in the second paragraph.

<u>WHEN THE PERTAMBOY CITY WAS BUILD, NO THOUGHT ABOUT THAT IN THE FUTURE THE POPULATION INCREASE FIVE TIMES MORE, NOW WE HAVE PROBLEM IN THE TRAFFIC AND IN THE PARKING GARAGE.</u>
<u>THE CITY MUST MAKE WIDER STREETS AND MORE PARKING GARAGES AND. IN THE BUSY INTERSECTIONS BUILD BRIDGES.</u>

4 *Transportation in Hong Kong*

A How many kinds of public transportation do you have in your city?
Does your city have any of the types in these pictures?

subway   tram   rickshaw   ferry

B Read about transportation in Hong Kong. Match the photos in part A
to the descriptions.

Getting Around Hong Kong

Hong Kong has an excellent transportation system, both old and new. If you fly there, you will arrive at one of the most modern airports in the world. And during your visit, there are many ways to get around Hong Kong.

1. _____

This word comes from the Japanese *jinrikisha*. It is a two-wheeled vehicle that is pulled by one person. Today, there are still about fifty of them in Hong Kong, but they are only for tourists.

2. _____

Take one of these to cross from Hong Kong Island to Kowloon or to visit one of the smaller islands. You can also use them to travel to Macau and Guangdong. They are safe and comfortable, and one of the cheapest boat rides in the world.

3. _____

Hong Kong's underground railway is called the MTR – the Mass Transit Railway. It is the fastest way to get around. Two tunnels cross under the harbor and go from Hong Kong Island to Kowloon.

4. _____

These are found on Hong Kong Island and take you to the top of Victoria Peak – 548 meters (1,800 feet) above sea level. The system is over a hundred years old. In that time, there has never been an accident. Two cars carry up to 120 passengers each.

C Which kind of transportation would you prefer to use? Why?

5 **Complete these conversations. Use words from the list.**

> ☑ bus station ☑ cash machine ☑ schedule
> ☑ duty-free shop ☐ sign

1. A: Could you tell me where I can buy some perfume?
   B: You should try the *duty-free shop* .

2. A: Can you tell me where the buses are?
   B: Yeah, there's a *BUS STATION* just
   outside this building.

3. A: Oh, no. I don't have enough money.
   B: There's a *CASH MACHINE* right over there.

4. A: Do you know what time the last bus leaves
   for downtown?
   B: No, but I can check the *SCHEDULE* for you.

5. A: Could you tell me where the taxi stand is?
   B: Sure. Just follow that *SIGN* .

6 **Complete the questions in this conversation at a hotel.**

Rob: Could you *tell me where the gym is* ?

Clerk: Sure, the gym is on the nineteenth floor.

Rob: OK. And can you *TELL ME WHERE THE COFFEE SHOP IS* ?

Clerk: Yes, the coffee shop is next to the gift shop.

Rob: The gift shop? Hmm. I need to buy something for my wife.
Do you *KNOW WHAT TIME THE GIFT SHOP CLOSE* ?

Clerk: It closes at six o'clock. I'm sorry, but you'll have to wait until
tomorrow. It's already six fifteen.

Rob: OK. Oh, I'm expecting a fax to arrive for me.
Could you *WHEN THE FAX ARRIVE* ?

Clerk: Don't worry. I'll call you when it arrives.

Rob: Thanks. Just one more thing.
Do you *KNOW WHEN DOES THE AIRPORT BUS LEAVE* ?

Clerk: The airport bus leaves every half hour. Anything else?

Rob: No, I don't think so. Thanks.

7 *Rewrite these sentences. Find another way to say each sentence using the words given.*

1. There are too many cars in this city. (fewer)

   There should be fewer cars in this city.

2. We need fewer buses and cars downtown. (traffic)

   THERE ARE TOO MUCH TRAFFIC IN THE DOWNTOWN.

3. Where's the subway entrance? (Could you)

   COULD YOU TELL ME WHERE THE SUBWAY ENTRANCE IS ?

4. There isn't enough public parking. (parking lots)

   THERE SHOULB BE MORE PARKIN LOTS

5. How often does the bus come? (Do you)

   DO YOU KNOW HOW OFTEN THE BUS COMES ?

6. What time does the last train leave? (Can you)

   CAN YOU TELL ME WHAT TIME THE LAST TRAIN LEAVES ?

---

8 *Answer these questions about your city or a city you know.*

The streets are
closed to cars in
a traffic–free zone.

1. Are there any traffic-free zones? Where are they located?

   YES, THERE ARE . THEY ARE LOCATED NEAR BY THE HISTORICAL CHURCH.

2. How do most people travel to and from work?

   THEY TRAVEL BY BUS .

3. What's rush hour like?

   IT IS TO BUSY .

4. What's the city's biggest problem?

   THE BIG

5. What has the city done about it?

6. Is there anything else the city could do?

3 Time for a change!

1 Write the opposites. Use the words from the list.

☐ dark   ☐ old
☐ expensive   ☐ safe
✓ inconvenient ☐ small
☐ noisy   ☐ spacious

1. convenient/_inconvenient_   5. light/_____

2. cramped/_____   6. modern/_____

3. dangerous/_____   7. quiet/_____

4. huge/_____   8. reasonable/_____

2 Rewrite these sentences. Find another way to say each sentence using not . . . enough or too and the words from part A.

1. The house is too expensive.

   The house isn't reasonable enough.

2. The rooms aren't light enough.

   _____

3. The living room isn't spacious enough for the family.

   _____

4. The bathroom is too old.

   _____

5. The yard isn't big enough for the children.

   _____

6. The street is too noisy for us.

   _____

7. The neighborhood is too dangerous.

   _____

8. The kitchen isn't convenient enough.

   _____

IT'S A BARGAIN!   FOR SALE

13

3 **Add the word enough to these sentences.**

> ### Grammar note: enough
>
> **Enough** comes __after__ adjectives but __before__ nouns.
>
> **adjective + enough**   **enough + noun**
> It isn't *spacious enough.*   There isn't *enough space.*
> The rooms aren't *light enough.*   It doesn't have *enough light.*

                    enough
1. The apartment isn't comfortable.ˆ   5. The neighborhood doesn't have street lights.

2. There aren't bedrooms.   6. There aren't closets.

3. It's not modern.   7. It's not private.

4. There aren't parking spaces.   8. The living room isn't spacious.

---

4 **Complete this conversation. Use the words given and the comparisons in the box. (Some of the comparisons in the box can be used more than once.)**

> just as many . . .   as many . . . as
> almost as . . . as   not as . . . as

Realtor: How did you like the house on Twelfth Street?

Lou: Well, it's ___not as convenient as___ the apartment

on Main Street. (convenient)

Realtor: That's true, the house is less convenient.

Lou: But the house is _____

the apartment. (cramped)

Realtor: Yes, the house is more spacious.

Lou: I think there are _____

in the apartment. (closets)

Realtor: You're right. The closet space is the same.

Lou: The wallpaper in the apartment is _____

_____ in the house. (shabby)

Realtor: I know, but you could change the wallpaper in the house.

Lou: Mmm, the rent on the apartment is _____

_____ the house, but the

house is much bigger. (expensive) Oh, I can't decide.

Can you show me something else?

5 *Home, sweet home*

A Complete this questionnaire about where you live and find your score below.

How does your home measure up?

The outside	Yes	No
1. Are you close enough to shopping?	☐	☐
2. Is there enough public transportation nearby?	☐	☐
3. Are the sidewalks clean?	☐	☐
4. Are there good restaurants in the neighborhood?	☐	☐
5. Is there a park nearby?	☐	☐
6. Is the neighborhood quiet?	☐	☐
7. Is the neighborhood safe?	☐	☐
8. Is there enough parking nearby?	☐	☐
9. Is the building in good condition?	☐	☐

The inside	Yes	No
10. Are there enough bedrooms?	☐	☐
11. Is there enough closet space?	☐	☐
12. Is the bathroom modern?	☐	☐
13. Is there a washing machine?	☐	☐
14. Is there enough space in the kitchen?	☐	☐
15. Do the stove and refrigerator work well?	☐	☐
16. Is the living room comfortable enough?	☐	☐
17. Is the dining area big enough?	☐	☐
18. Are the walls newly painted?	☐	☐
19. Are the rooms bright enough?	☐	☐
20. Is the building warm enough in winter?	☐	☐

To score:

How many "Yes" answers do you have?

16–20
It sounds like a dream home!

11–15
Great! All you need now is a swimming pool!

6–10
Well, at least houseguests won't want to stay too long!

0–5
Time to look for a better place to live!

B Write two short paragraphs about where you live. In the first paragraph describe your neighborhood, and in the second paragraph describe your home. Use the information in part A or information of your own.

_____

_____

_____

_____

_____

_____

6 *Collocations*

A Which words or phrases often go with which verbs? Complete the chart.

☐ my appearance   ☐ happier   ☐ no homework   ☐ my job
☐ more free time   ☑ healthier   ☐ somewhere else   ☐ to a new place

be	change	have	move
healthier			

B Describe what these people would like to change. Use *I wish* and words or phrases from part A.

1. *I wish I were healthier.*   2. _____

3. _____   4. _____

5. _____   6. _____

7 *Wish list*

A Find six things Dan would like to change in his life.
Write sentences with *He wishes*.

I used to enjoy life more. Nowadays, I just go to work in the morning and come home in the evening. I don't enjoy my job anymore, but I must say the money is good. I don't go out as often as I used to. I used to go to the movies once a week. Now I go to the movies only once a month. And I used to visit my friends all the time. Now I never see them. My weekends are really boring, too. I spend my time cleaning the house and watching TV. Why don't I go out more often? I guess I just got lazy. Perhaps I should buy a car. Yeah, I've saved a lot of money. I'll go buy a new car right now!

1. *He wishes he enjoyed his job.* _____

2. _____

3. _____

4. _____

5. _____

6. _____

B Write a wish list. Put your wishes in order of importance (1 = very important;
5 = not very important).

1. _____

2. _____

3. _____

4. _____

5. _____

8 *Choose the correct responses.*

1. A: I wish I could change my lifestyle.

   B: *Why?* _____

   - Why?
   - I don't like my job, either.

2. A: I wish I could retire.

   B: _____

   - I don't like it anymore.
   - I know what you mean.

3. A: Where do you want to move?

   B: _____

   - Somewhere else.
   - Something else.

4. A: I wish I could find a bigger apartment.

   B: _____

   - Is it too large?
   - I like it, though.

9 *Rewrite these sentences. Find another way to say each sentence using the words given.*

1. There should be more bedrooms. (enough)

   There aren't enough bedrooms. _____

2. The neighborhood is safe enough. (dangerous)

   _____

3. My apartment doesn't have enough privacy. (private)

   _____

4. Our house has the same number of bedrooms as yours. (just as many)

   _____

5. I don't have enough closet space. (wish)

   _____

6. We wish we could move to a new place. (somewhere else)

   _____

7. The apartment is too small. (big)

   _____

8. I wish this exercise were easy. (not difficult)

   _____

4 I've never heard of that!

1 *Complete this conversation with the correct tense.*

Isabel: I went to Sunrise Beach last week.

Have you ever been to Sunrise Beach, Andy?
(Did you ever go/Have you ever been)

Andy: Yes, _____ . It's beautiful.
(I did/I have)

_____ there on the weekend?
(Did you go/Have you gone)

Isabel: Yeah, I _____ . I _____
(did/have)   (went/have gone)

on Sunday. _____
(I got up/I've gotten up)

at 4:00 A.M.

Andy: Wow! _____
(I never woke up/I've never woken up)

that early!

Isabel: Oh, it wasn't so bad. I _____
(got/have gotten)

to the beach early to see the sun rise.

_____ a
(Did you ever see/Have you ever seen)

sunrise, Andy?

Andy: No, _____ . I prefer sunsets to sunrises.
(I didn't/I haven't)

Isabel: Really? Then I _____ swimming
(went/have gone)

around 6:00, but there were some strange dark shadows

in the water. _____ of sharks at Sunrise Beach?
(Did you ever hear/Have you ever heard)

Andy: Yes, _____ . I _____ a news report about sharks last summer.
(I did/I have)   (heard/have heard)

Isabel: Gee! Maybe I _____ a lucky escape on Sunday morning! Why don't you
(had/have had)

come with me next time?

Andy: Are you kidding?

2 *Have you ever . . . ?*

A Look at this list and check (✓) five things you have done. Add your own ideas if necessary.

☐	eat raw fish
☐	have green tea ice cream
☐	try Indian food
☐	cook for over ten people
☐	go horseback riding
☐	read a novel in English
☐	go to a rock concert
☐	travel abroad
☐	take a cruise
☐	ride a motorcycle
☐	_____
☐	_____
☐	_____
☐	_____

B Write questions about the things you checked in part A. Use *Have you ever . . . ?*

1. *Have you ever had green tea ice cream?*

2. _____

3. _____

4. _____

5. _____

C Answer the questions you wrote in part B. Then use the past tense to give more information.

1. *Yes, I have. I had some in a Japanese restaurant. It was delicious.*

2. _____

3. _____

4. _____

5. _____

3 Do I have a food allergy?

A If a kind of food always makes you feel sick in some way, it may mean you have a food allergy. Do you have any food allergies? If so, what shouldn't you eat? What happens if you eat it?

B Read about these people with food allergies.

Food Allergies

Luis always had headaches and stomachaches. First, Luis's doctor gave him some medicine, but it didn't work. Then his doctor asked him about his favorite foods. Luis said he loved cakes and ice cream. His doctor said, "Stop eating sweets." Luis stopped, but he still got headaches and stomachaches. Next, his doctor asked more questions about his diet. Luis said he ate a lot of fish. His doctor said to stop eating fish. When Luis stopped eating fish, he felt much better.

Sharon often had a very sore mouth after eating. First, she stopped drinking milk and eating cheese, but this made no difference. Then, in the summer, the problem became really bad, and it was difficult for Sharon to eat. Her doctor asked about her diet. She said she had a tomato garden, and she ate about ten tomatoes a day. Sharon's doctor told her not to eat tomatoes. When she stopped eating tomatoes, Sharon's mouth got better.

Fred is a mechanic, but he was not able to hold his tools. His hands were swollen. First, he went to his doctor, and she gave him some medicine. The medicine didn't work. He still couldn't hold his tools. After that, his doctor asked him about his diet. Fred told her he ate a lot of bread. She told him not to eat bread or pasta. After ten days, Fred could hold his tools again.

C Complete the chart.

	Problem	What didn't work	What worked
Luis			
Sharon			
Fred			

4 Eggs, anyone?

A Here's a recipe for a mushroom omelet. Look at the pictures and number the sentences from 1 to 5.

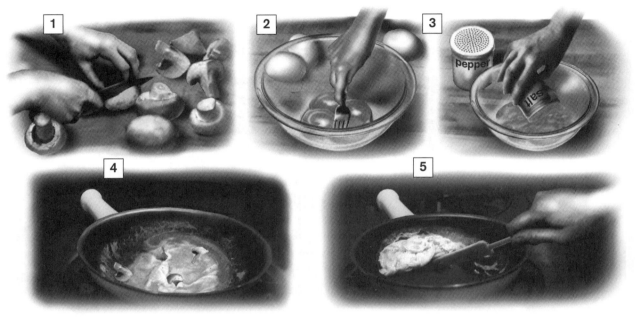

_____ After that, pour the eggs into a frying pan. Add the mushrooms and cook.

_____ Then beat the eggs in a bowl.

_1_ First, slice the mushrooms.

_____ Next, add salt and pepper to the egg mixture.

_____ Finally, fold the omelet in half. And enjoy! Your omelet is ready!

B Describe your favorite way to cook eggs. Use sequence adverbs.

How to cook _____

5

Complete the conversation. Use the past tense or the present perfect of the words given.

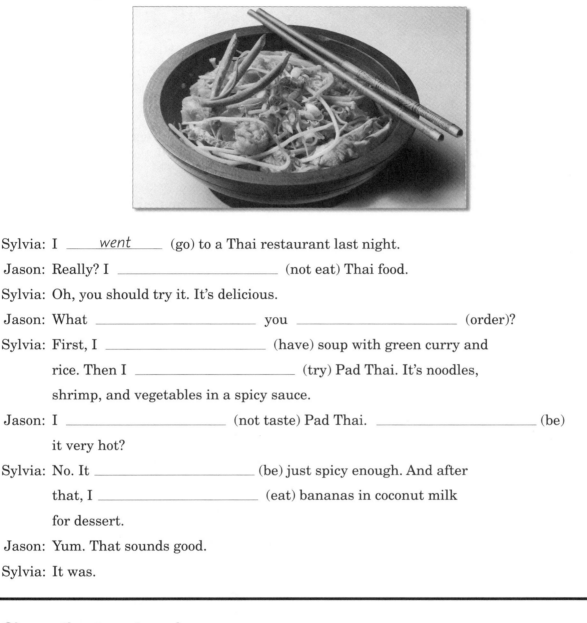

Sylvia: I ____went____ (go) to a Thai restaurant last night.

Jason: Really? I _____ (not eat) Thai food.

Sylvia: Oh, you should try it. It's delicious.

Jason: What _____ you _____ (order)?

Sylvia: First, I _____ (have) soup with green curry and

rice. Then I _____ (try) Pad Thai. It's noodles,

shrimp, and vegetables in a spicy sauce.

Jason: I _____ (not taste) Pad Thai. _____ (be)

it very hot?

Sylvia: No. It _____ (be) just spicy enough. And after

that, I _____ (eat) bananas in coconut milk

for dessert.

Jason: Yum. That sounds good.

Sylvia: It was.

6

Choose the correct word.

1. We had delicious guacamole dip and chips on Saturday night. It was a

   great ____snack____ (dinner/snack/marinade).

2. I had a huge lunch, so I _____ (ordered/skipped/tried) dinner.

3. What _____ (appetizers/ingredients/skewers) do

   you need to cook crispy fried noodles?

4. First, fry the beef in oil and curry powder and then _____

   (pour/put/spread) the coconut milk over the beef.

5. We need to leave the restaurant soon. Could we have the

   _____ (bill/bowl/menu), please?

7 Choose the correct responses.

| ☐ Yuck! That sounds awful. | ☐ That sounds strange. | ☐ Mmm! That sounds good. |

1. A: Have you ever tried barbecued fish? You marinate the fish in soy
   sauce and garlic for about an hour and then barbecue it.

   B: _____

2. A: Here's a recipe called Baked Eggplant Delight. I usually bake eggplant for
   an hour, but this says you bake the eggplant for only ten minutes.

   B: _____

3. A: Look at this dish – frog's legs with bananas! I've never seen that on
   a menu before.

   B: _____

8 Use these verbs to complete the crossword puzzle. Use the past tense or the present perfect.

| ✔ be | ☐ bring | ☐ decide | ☐ drive | ☐ forget | ☐ have | ☐ ride | ☐ take |
| ☐ break | ☐ buy | ☐ do | ☐ eat | ☐ give | ☐ make | ☐ skip | ☐ try |

Across

1 We have never ____ to a Chinese restaurant.

3 I ____ all the ingredients with me.

7 ____ you eat a huge dinner last night?

8 We ____ my mother to the new Chilean restaurant.

11 I haven't ____ a birthday gift to my father yet.

12 Have you ever ____ a horse? It's great!

13 I have never ____ snails. What are they like?

14 Have you ____ what kind of pizza you would like?

Down

1 I ____ this chicken for $5.

2 Oh, I'm sorry. I just ____ a glass.

4 Victor ____ Chinese chicken for dinner.

5 I wasn't hungry this morning, so I ____ breakfast.

6 Oh, no! I ____ to buy rice.

7 Have you ever ____ a sports car?

9 I ____ Greek food for the first time last night.

10 Have you ever ____ Peruvian Ceviche? It's delicious.

5 Going places

1 Collocations

A Which words or phrases often go with which verbs? Complete the chart. Use each word or phrase only once.

- ☐ a camper
- ☐ camping
- ☐ a car
- ☐ my studying
- ☐ a condominium
- ☑ long walks
- ☐ lots of hiking
- ☐ my reading
- ☐ sailing lessons
- ☐ my homework
- ☐ some fishing
- ☐ something exciting
- ☐ swimming
- ☐ a vacation
- ☐ on vacation

take	rent	go
long walks		

catch up on	do

B Write four things you plan to do on your next vacation. Use *going to* and the information in part A or your own information.

Vacation plans

1. _____
2. _____
3. _____
4. _____

C Write four sentences about your possible vacation plans. Use *will* with *maybe*, *probably*, *I guess*, or *I think*. Use the information in part A or your own information.

Vacation possibilities

1. _____
2. _____
3. _____
4. _____

2 Complete the conversation. Use going to or will and the information on the notepads.

Dave: So, Stella, do you have any vacation plans?

Stella: Well, _I'm going to paint my apartment_ . The walls
are a really ugly color. What about you? Are you going
to do anything special?

Dave: _____ and take a long drive.

Stella: Where are you going to go?

Dave: I'm not sure. _____ .
I haven't seen her in a long time.

Stella: That sounds nice. I always like to visit my family.

Dave: Yes, and _____ for a
few days. I haven't been hiking in months. How about you?
Are you going to do anything else on your vacation?

Stella: _____ . I have a lot
of work to do before school starts.

Dave: That doesn't sound like much fun.

Stella: Oh, I am planning to have some fun.
_____ . I love to swim.

Stella's Pad

paint my apartment - yes

catch up on my
studying - probably

relax on the beach - yes

DAVE'S PAD

rent a car - yes

visit my sister
Joanne - probably

go to the
mountains - maybe

3 Travel plans

A Look at these answers. Write questions using *going to*.

1. A: _Where are you going to go?_
   B: I'm going to go someplace nice and quiet.

2. A: _____
   B: I'm going to drive.

3. A: _____
   B: I'm going to stay in a condominium. My friend has one near the beach.

4. A: _____
   B: No, I'm going to travel by myself.

B Use the cues to write other answers to the questions in part A.

1. _I'm not going to go to a busy place._   (not go/busy place)

2. _____   (maybe/take the train)

3. _____   (not stay/hotel)

4. _____   (I think/ask a friend)

4 Travel ads

A Do you ever read travel ads? Have you ever taken a vacation after reading an ad? If so, how was the vacation?

B Read this travel ad.

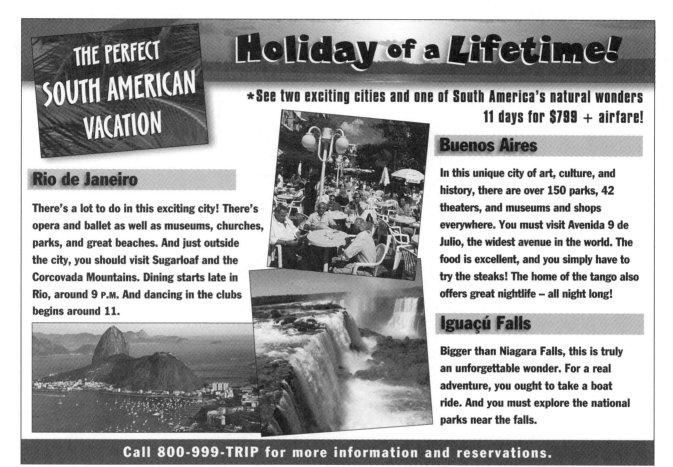

THE PERFECT SOUTH AMERICAN VACATION

Holiday of a Lifetime!

*See two exciting cities and one of South America's natural wonders
11 days for $799 + airfare!

Rio de Janeiro

There's a lot to do in this exciting city! There's opera and ballet as well as museums, churches, parks, and great beaches. And just outside the city, you should visit Sugarloaf and the Corcovada Mountains. Dining starts late in Rio, around 9 P.M. And dancing in the clubs begins around 11.

Buenos Aires

In this unique city of art, culture, and history, there are over 150 parks, 42 theaters, and museums and shops everywhere. You must visit Avenida 9 de Julio, the widest avenue in the world. The food is excellent, and you simply have to try the steaks! The home of the tango also offers great nightlife – all night long!

Iguaçú Falls

Bigger than Niagara Falls, this is truly an unforgettable wonder. For a real adventure, you ought to take a boat ride. And you must explore the national parks near the falls.

Call 800-999-TRIP for more information and reservations.

C Check (✓) True or False. For the statements that are false, write the true information.

	True	False
1. People have dinner late in Rio de Janeiro.	☐	☐
2. Niagara Falls is bigger than Iguaçú Falls.	☐	☐
3. Both Rio de Janeiro and Buenos Aires have an exciting nightlife.	☐	☐
4. Rio de Janeiro, Iguaçú Falls, and Buenos Aires have unforgettable parks and beaches.	☐	☐

5 *Circle the correct word or words to give advice to travelers.*

1. You ought (check / (to check)) the weather.

2. You should never (leave / to leave) cash in your hotel room.

3. You need (take / to take) your credit card with you.

4. You have (pay / to pay) an airport tax.

5. You should (let / to let) your family know where they can contact you.

6. You'd better not (go / to go) out alone late at night.

7. You must (get / to get) a vaccination if you go to some countries.

8. You don't have (get / to get) a visa for many countries nowadays.

6 *Take it or leave it?*

A Check (✓) the most important item to have in each situation.

1. A vacation to a foreign country
   - ☐ an overnight bag
   - ✓ a passport
   - ☐ a driver's license

2. A mountain-climbing vacation
   - ☐ a suitcase
   - ☐ a visa
   - ☐ a windbreaker

3. A sailing trip
   - ☐ a hotel reservation
   - ☐ a first-aid kit
   - ☐ hiking boots

4. A visit to a temple
   - ☐ a credit card
   - ☐ suitable clothes
   - ☐ a plane ticket

B Give advice to these people. Use the words or phrases in the box and the items in part A. Use each word or phrase only once.

> ☐ ought to   ☐ need to
> ☐ should   ✓ had better ('d better)

1. Norma is going on a vacation to a foreign country.

   She'd better take a passport.

2. June and Steven are going on a mountain-climbing vacation.

   _____

3. Philip and Julia are planning a sailing trip.

   _____

4. Jack is going to visit a temple.

   _____

7 *You don't need to take that!*

Your friends are planning to drive across North America and camp along the way. What advice can you give them? Write eight sentences using the expressions in the box and some of the cues below.

> You have to . . .
> You must . . .
> You need to . . .
> You don't have to . . .
> You'd better . . .
> You should . . .
> You shouldn't . . .
> You ought to . . .

take your driver's license
buy good quality camping equipment
take cooking equipment
forget your passport or identification
take a credit card
pack a lot of luggage

remember to bring a jacket
forget a first-aid kit
take a lot of cash
take maps and travel guides
remember to bring insect spray

1. *You have to take your driver's license.*
2. _____
3. _____
4. _____
5. _____
6. _____
7. _____
8. _____

8 *Rewrite these sentences. Find another way to say each sentence using the words given.*

1. I'm not going to go on vacation on my own. (alone)

   _____

2. I don't want to travel with anyone. (by myself)

   _____

3. You ought to travel with a friend. (should)

   _____

4. You have to take warm clothes. (must)

   _____

9 *I'm going on vacation!*

A Read these notes for a vacation you are going to take to Portugal and Spain. Then write a description of your vacation. Use *going to* for the plans that you have decided on. Use *will* with *maybe, probably, I guess,* or *I think* for the plans you are not sure about.

First, I'm going to arrive in Lisbon, Portugal, on July 6th. I'm going to

check in at the Tivoli Hotel. Then maybe I'll go shopping. . . .

_____

_____

_____

_____

_____

_____

_____

B Write five things you need to remember before you go on vacation.

1. *I have to pick up my plane ticket.* _____

2. _____

3. _____

4. _____

5. _____

6 Sure. No problem!

1 **Write responses to these requests. Use *it* or them.**

1. Please take out the trash.
   OK, I'll take it out.

2. Please put the dishes away.
   _____

3. Hang up the towels.
   _____

4. Turn off the lights, please.
   _____

5. Turn on the radio.
   _____

2 *Two-part verbs*

A Use words from the list to make two-part verbs. (You will use words more than once.)

away	down	off	on	out	up

1. clean __*up*__   6. take _____
2. clean _____   7. take _____
3. hang _____   8. pick _____
4. put _____   9. turn _____
5. put _____   10. turn _____

B Make requests with two-part verbs in part A. Then give a reason for making the request.

1. *Please clean up your room. It's dirty.* _____
2. _____
3. _____
4. _____
5. _____

3 *Choose the correct words.*

1. Hang up your ___pants___ . (books/pants/trash)

2. Take out the _____ . (oven/trash/yard)

3. Turn down the _____ . (cigarette/heat/toys)

4. Pick up your _____ . (light/things/TV)

5. Put away your _____ . (clothes/faucet/yard)

6. Turn on the _____ . (cat/mess/radio)

4 *What's your excuse?*

A Complete these requests with a sentence from the list.

☐ It's a mess.　　☑ They shouldn't be on the floor.
☐ It's too loud.　☐ The milk is getting warm.
☐ They're dirty.

1. Pick up your clothes, please. *They shouldn't be on the floor.*

2. Please put the groceries away. _____

3. Take your shoes off. _____

4. Clean up the kitchen, please. _____

5. Turn down the music. _____

B Write an excuse for each request in part A.

1. *Sorry, but there isn't enough room in my closet.*

2. _____

3. _____

4. _____

5. _____

5 *The power of persuasion*

A How do you make a request? What do you do when someone says "no"?

B Read this article.

Persuasion Strategies

In many situations, people try to persuade others to do things; however, most people are not aware of how they persuade. Three different strategies are often used by couples and by people in business: a **"hard"** strategy, a **"soft"** strategy, and a **"fair"** strategy.

Strategy	Couples	Managers
Hard	• I get angry and make the other person give in. • Well, first, I try to make the other person feel stupid. • I say I'll leave if my spouse does not agree.	• I just order the person to do what I ask. • I say that I won't give the person a good report on his or her work. • I get others to support my request.
Soft	• I act warm and charming before I bring up the subject. • I am so nice that the other person cannot refuse.	• I act very humble while I'm making my request. • I make the person feel important by saying that she or he has the brains and experience to do what I want.
Fair	• I say I'll give up a little if the other person gives up a little. • We discuss our views without arguing.	• I offer to exchange favors: You do this for me and I'll do something for you. • I explain the reason for my request.

C Look at what these people say. Are they examples of hard, soft, or fair strategies?

1. Wife to husband: Hey, honey. You know, you make the very best coffee. Could I have a cup of that terrific coffee?

   Strategy: _____

2. Father to daughter: Pick up that mess in your room, right now. Can't you do anything right?

   Strategy: _____

3. Boss to secretary: I need you to stay late tonight to finish a report. But you can leave work early tomorrow. Is that OK?

   Strategy: _____

D Which strategy do you use most often?
Which strategy do you think is the most effective?

6 *Rewrite these sentences. Find another way to say each sentence using the words given.*

1. Take your feet off my chair. (Can)

   Can you take your feet off my chair, please?

2. Take this form to the office. (Would you mind)

   _____

3. Please turn the CD player down. (Could)

   _____

4. Don't leave the door open. (Would you mind)

   _____

5. Let me share your book. (Would)

   _____

6. Pass me that book, please. (Can)

   _____

7 *Choose the correct responses.*

1. A: Could you lend me some money?

   B: *Oh, sure.* _____
   - Oh, sure.
   - Oh, sorry.
   - No, thanks.

2. A: Would you mind helping me?

   B: _____
   - Sorry, I can't right now.
   - No, thanks.
   - I forget.

3. A: By the way, you're sitting in my seat.

   B: _____
   - I'll close it.
   - Not right now.
   - Excuse me. I didn't realize.

4. A: Would you like to come in?

   B: _____
   - That's no excuse.
   - Sorry, I forgot.
   - All right. Thanks.

5. A: Would you mind not taking all the coffee?

   B: _____
   - OK, thanks.
   - I'm sorry, I'll make some more.
   - Excuse me. I'll drink it all.

6. A: Can you turn the radio up?

   B: _____
   - No problem.
   - You could, too.
   - I'll make sure.

8 *For each complaint, apologize and either make an offer, give an excuse, admit a mistake, or make a promise.*

1. Customer: This steak is very tough. I can't eat it.

   Waiter: *Oh, I'm sorry. I'll get you another one.*

2. Steven: You're late. I've been waiting for you for half an hour.

   Katie: _____

3. Roommate 1: Could you turn the television down?
   I'm trying to study and the noise is bothering me.

   Roommate 2: _____

4. Father: You didn't mail the letters this morning.

   Son: _____

5. Customer: I brought this Walkman in for repair last week,
   but it's still not working right.

   Salesperson: _____

6. Neighbor 1: Could you do something about your dog?
   It barks all night and keeps me awake.

   Neighbor 2: _____

7. Apartment resident: Would you mind moving your car?
   You're parked in my parking space.

   Visitor: _____

8. Teacher: Please put away your papers. You left them on
   your desk yesterday.

   Student: _____

9 *Choose the correct words.*

1. Throw those empty bottles away. Put them in the
   _____ (recycling bin/toy/refrigerator).

2. Would you mind picking up some _____
   (dry cleaning/groceries/towels)? We need coffee, milk, and rice.

3. Turn the _____ (faucet/oven/stereo) off. Water
   costs money!

4. My neighbor made a _____ (mistake/offer/promise).
   He said, "I'll be sure to stop my dog from barking."

10 Requests

A Match the phrases in columns A and B.

A	B	
☑ pick up	☐ your bedroom	**1.** *pick up some milk*
☐ not criticize	☑ some milk	**2.** _____
☐ mail	☐ the videotapes	**3.** _____
☐ not talk	☐ your sunglasses	**4.** _____
☐ put away	☐ these letters	**5.** _____
☐ take off	☐ the oven	**6.** _____
☐ turn down	☐ so loud	**7.** _____
☐ clean up	☐ my friends	**8.** _____

B Write requests using the phrases from part A.

1. *Would you mind picking up some milk?* _____
2. _____
3. _____
4. _____
5. _____
6. _____
7. _____
8. _____

11 Write five complaints you have about a friend or relative. Then write a wish for each complaint.

1. *My roommate Linda is always using my hair dryer.*
   I wish she would buy her own hair dryer.

2. _____
   _____

3. _____
   _____

4. _____
   _____

5. _____
   _____

7 What's this for?

1

What are these items used for? Write a sentence about each item using used for and information from the list.

- ☐ do boring jobs
- ☑ write reports
- ☐ talk to friends
- ☐ send documents
- ☐ transmit radio and TV programs

1	2	3	4	5
computer	fax machine	robot	satellite	telephone

1. _A computer is used for writing reports._
2. _____
3. _____
4. _____
5. _____

2

Find the connection between two of these words. Check (✓) the technology and check (✓) what it does. Then write a sentence using used to.

1. ☑ e-mail   ☑ phone line   ☐ TV programs
   A phone line is used to send e-mail.

2. ☐ CD-ROM   ☐ Xerox machine   ☐ photocopies
   _____

3. ☐ budgets   ☐ satellites   ☐ weather
   _____

4. ☐ criminals   ☐ DNA fingerprinting   ☐ tasks
   _____

5. ☐ the World Wide Web   ☐ robots   ☐ information
   _____

3 *Choose the correct words to complete each sentence.*
Use the correct form of the word.

1. Robots are used to ____*perform*____ (make/perform/study) many
   dangerous jobs.

2. CD-ROM is used for _____ (connect/perform/store)
   information on many subjects.

3. Police use DNA fingerprinting to _____ (identify/
   read/transmit) criminals.

4. Computers are used to _____ (access/do/send) the Internet.

5. Satellites are used for _____ (make/
   transmit/write) radio programs.

6. Home computers are used to _____ (do/make/have) budgets.

4 *Complete the sentences with* **used to,** *is* **used to,** *or* **are used to.**

1. My sister _____*used to*_____ belong to a "chat group" on astronomy.

2. People always _____ mail letters, but nowadays they
   often fax them.

3. A cellular phone _____ make phone calls from cars or
   from the street.

4. I _____ have an electric typewriter, but now I have
   a computer.

5. We just bought a great new CD player. We _____ have
   a cassette player, but it was terrible.

6. Modems _____ access the Internet.

5 *Garage sales*

A Have you ever been to a garage sale? What did you buy?
Do you have garage sales in your country?

B Read these advertisements for garage sales.

A HOUSEHOLD goods, including refrigerator, dishwasher, microwave oven, TV, stereo, couch, 2 bikes. Sat. 9–3. 1528 Williams Dr. Remember to bring cash only!

B *MOVING!* Typewriter, books, shelves, desk and office chair, and lots of old CDs! Sat. 8–3. 32 Harbor Rd.

C *VALUABLE* Mexican paintings, antique chairs, oriental rugs, collection of old Japanese kimonos and other clothes from around the world, old maps, gold coins. Sun. 11–5. 2039 E. 8th St. Try not to be late.

D COLLECTOR GOES BROKE! Everything must go! Collection of shells, stamps, and coins from around the world, old postcards, photos. Sun. noon to 7. 9734 Date St. Make sure to tell your friends.

E *ELECTRICAL* engineer retiring. Laptop computer, modem, laser printer, fax machine, software for word processing and making budgets, even a few video games. 9–5 Sat. & Sun. 2561 Canada Dr.

C Which garage sale should these people attend? (More than one answer is sometimes possible.)

1. _____ Linda has just started her own business. She likes to play music while she works.

2. _____ Edmund and Tom decorate homes. They always use old and unusual items to make the houses they decorate more interesting.

3. _____ Don needs some furniture for his new apartment.

4. _____ Betty wants to have an office in her home.

5. _____ Sam likes collecting interesting and unusual things from different countries.

6 ***What are they usually used for?***

A Complete the word map with inventions from the list.
(Some of the inventions can be used in more than one category.)

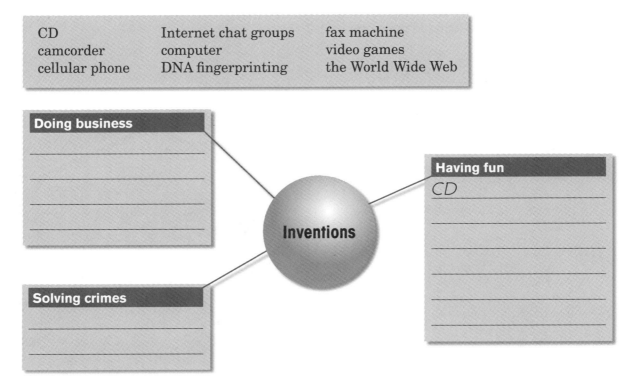

CD	Internet chat groups	fax machine
camcorder	computer	video games
cellular phone	DNA fingerprinting	the World Wide Web

Doing business

Inventions

Having fun
CD

Solving crimes

B Do you use any of these inventions? What do you use them for? Write sentences.

1. *I use a cellular phone to call my office.*
2. _____
3. _____
4. _____

7 ***Put these instructions in order. Number them from 1 to 5.***

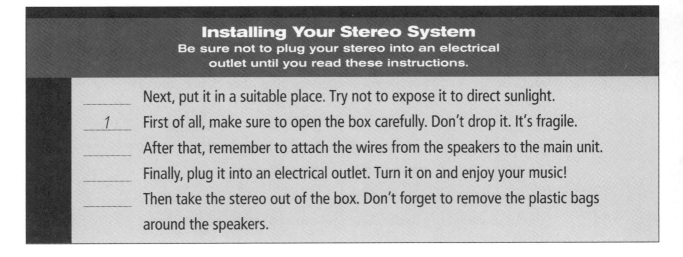

Installing Your Stereo System
Be sure not to plug your stereo into an electrical
outlet until you read these instructions.

_____	Next, put it in a suitable place. Try not to expose it to direct sunlight.
1	First of all, make sure to open the box carefully. Don't drop it. It's fragile.
_____	After that, remember to attach the wires from the speakers to the main unit.
_____	Finally, plug it into an electrical outlet. Turn it on and enjoy your music!
_____	Then take the stereo out of the box. Don't forget to remove the plastic bags around the speakers.

8 *Write sentences about these pictures using expressions from the list.*

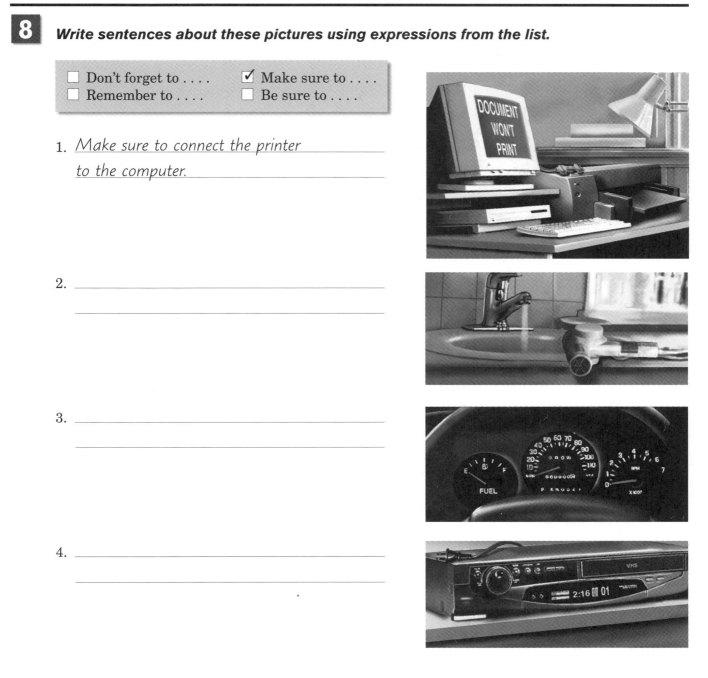

☐ Don't forget to . . . .   ☑ Make sure to . . . .
☐ Remember to . . . .   ☐ Be sure to . . . .

1. *Make sure to connect the printer to the computer.*

2. _____

3. _____

4. _____

9 *Write a or an in the correct places. (Find nine other places where you need to do so.)*

My brother just bought ^a^ laptop computer. It's really great. It has color screen; it is easier on the eyes than black-and-white screen. The computer has battery, so he can use it without electricity for up to eight hours. It also has modem inside. If he wants to send fax, he can send it electronically. And he can connect to the Internet. My brother joined "chat group" on mountain climbing. He plans to take his laptop on airplane when he takes vacation mountain climbing. It's very small computer, so he takes it everywhere with him.

10 *Rewrite these sentences. Find another way to say each sentence using the words given.*

1. I use my computer for organizing my money. (budget)

    I use my computer for making my budget.

2. It breaks very easily. (fragile)

    _____

3. Take it out of the outlet. (unplug)

    _____

4. Remember to keep it dry. (spill)

    _____

5. Don't drop the package. (try not to)

    _____

11 *Look at the pictures and complete this conversation. Choose the correct responses.*

A: What a day! First, my microwave oven didn't work.

B: What happened?

A: *It burned my lunch.*
   - It didn't cook my lunch.
   - It burned my lunch.

   Then I tried to use my computer,

   but that didn't work either.

B: Why not?

A: _____
   - It didn't connect to the Internet.
   - I couldn't turn it on.

   After that I tried to use the vacuum cleaner.

B: Let me guess. It didn't pick up the dirt.

A: Worse! _____
   - It made a terrible noise.
   - It spread dirt around the room.

B: Did you have your robot help?

A: Well, I tried to get it to clean the outside

   windows. _____
   - But it refused.
   - It did a great job.

B: I don't blame it! You live on the 50th floor!

8 Let's celebrate!

1 Complete this paragraph with words from the list.

- ☐ fall
- ☐ families
- ☐ fireworks
- ☐ harvest
- ☐ holidays
- ☐ independence
- ☑ July
- ☐ picnics
- ☐ roast

Two of the most important holidays in the United States are Independence Day and Thanksgiving Day. Independence Day, the Fourth of ___July___ , marks the United States' declaration of _____ from Britain. Most towns, big and small, celebrate the Fourth of July with parades and _____ . Families celebrate with

Independence Day parade

barbecues or _____ . Thanksgiving Day is celebrated in the _____ , on the fourth Thursday in November. It is a day when people give thanks for the _____ . Most _____ have a large dinner with _____ turkey. Both Thanksgiving and Independence Day are national _____ .

2 Complete the sentences. Choose clauses from the list.

- ☐ when I feel sad and depressed
- ☐ when school starts
- ☐ when people pay taxes
- ☐ when students in the United States take exams

1. I hate April 15th! In the United States, it's the day _____
_____ . I owe the government money every year.

2. I don't like September. It's the month _____ .
I always miss summer vacation.

3. June is my least favorite month. It's the month _____
_____ . I never study enough.

4. I have never liked winter. It's a season _____ .
The cold weather always affects my mood.

43

3 *Complete the crossword puzzle.*

Across

4 People in the United States and Canada celebrate the _____ at Thanksgiving.

7 Children say "trick or treat" on Halloween, and people give them _____ .

8 _____ is the season when there are a lot of flowers in my country.

10 My parents' twenty-fifth wedding _____ is tomorrow.

13 _____ is a time of the year when it is very cold and dark.

14 During Carnival, people wear lots of interesting _____ .

15 My wife loves _____ , so I gave her a diamond ring on Valentine's Day.

16 My family always has a _____ in the park on Independence Day.

17 We have a summer festival when everyone goes _____ in the streets. It's fun, and the music is great, too.

Down

1 People like to play _____ on each other on April Fool's Day.

2 Everybody wore a _____ on Halloween, so no one knew who was really at the party.

3 Janice and Nick are getting married soon. They plan to have a small _____ with just a few family members.

5 In my country, most people have roast _____ on Christmas Day.

6 August 1st is the day when Indonesians celebrate their _____ from the Netherlands.

9 On July 14th each year, the French celebrate their _____ with fireworks.

11 In Europe, summer is the _____ when most people go on vacation.

12 We always have a _____ on New Year's Eve.

14 The Chinese eat special _____ for the moon festival. These are sweet and are made with lots of eggs.

4 *A lot to celebrate!*

A Do you know about any special days in the United States?
Which days do you know about?

B Read about these special days in the United States.

	Event	Day	How people celebrate it
	Easter	a Sunday in March or April	For Christians, this is a religious holiday. It is also a day when many people buy chocolate eggs and bunnies and have Easter egg hunts outdoors.
	Secretaries' Day	April	When secretaries come to work, their bosses give them cards and flowers.
	Earth Day	April 22	This is a day when people think about protecting the earth. People give speeches about saving the environment.
	Mother's Day	2nd Sunday in May	People honor their mothers by giving cards and gifts and having a family gathering.
	Father's Day	3rd Sunday in June	People honor their fathers by giving them presents and cards.
	Labor Day	1st Monday in September	People honor workers and have picnics with family and friends.
	Hanukkah	usually in December	During this religious festival, Jewish families light candles and give each other gifts.
	Christmas	December 25	For Christians, this is a religious holiday. It is also a day when friends and families exchange gifts around a Christmas tree.

C Complete the chart. Check (✓) the correct answers.

	People give gifts on:	The religious holidays are:	I celebrate:
Easter	☐	☐	☐
Secretaries' Day	☐	☐	☐
Earth Day	☐	☐	☐
Mother's Day	☐	☐	☐
Father's Day	☐	☐	☐
Labor Day	☐	☐	☐
Hanukkah	☐	☐	☐
Christmas	☐	☐	☐

5 What happens at these times in your country? Complete the sentences.

1. Before a man and woman get married, _they_ _usually date each other._ .

2. When someone has a birthday, _____ _____ .

3. Before some people eat a meal, _____ _____ .

4. After a student graduates, _____ _____ .

5. When a woman gets engaged, _____ _____ .

6. When a couple has their first child, _____ _____ .

7. When a person retires, _____ _____ .

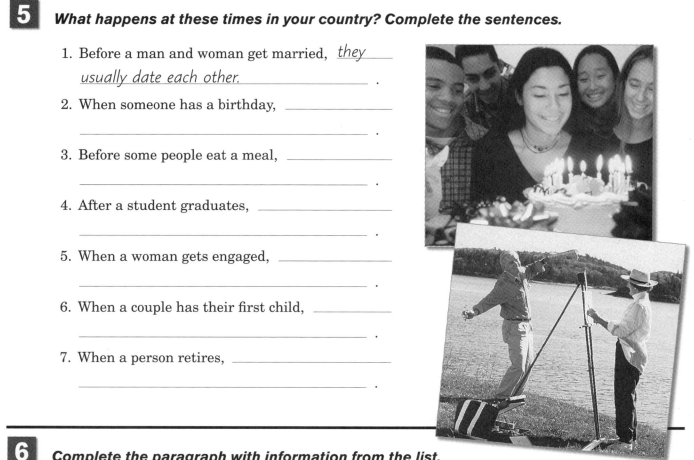

6 Complete the paragraph with information from the list. Add a comma where necessary.

> **Grammar note: Adverbial clauses of time**
>
> The adverbial clause can come before or after the main clause.
>
> **Before the main clause, add a comma.**
> *When a couple gets married*, they often receive gifts.
>
> **After the main clause, do not add a comma.**
> A couple often receives gifts *when they get married*.

☐ many newlyweds have to live with relatives
☐ before the wedding reception ends
☐ they like to be alone
☐ when they have enough money to pay for it

Newly married couples often leave on their honeymoon_____
_____ . When they go on their
honeymoon_____ .
After they come back from their honeymoon_____
_____ . They can only live in a place of their
own_____ .

7   *Choose the correct words or phrases.*

1. In the United States, when a man and woman decide to get engaged,
   they send ___*announcements*___ (announcements/gifts/receptions)
   to their friends.

2. The woman's female friends often give her _____ (a bridal shower/
   an engagement period/newlyweds).

3. The man's male friends often give him a _____ (bachelor party/
   bridegroom/wedding dress).

4. The wedding _____ (anniversary/celebrations/ceremony)
   is often held in a church.

5. After the wedding reception, the couple usually goes on their
   _____ (engagement/honeymoon/vacation).

8   *Write three paragraphs about marriage customs in your country.*
In the first paragraph, write about what happens before the wedding.
In the second paragraph, write about the wedding ceremony.
In the final paragraph, write about what happens after the wedding.

_____

_____

_____

_____

_____

_____

_____

_____

Japan   the United States   Cambodia   Suriname

9   *Rewrite these sentences. Find another way to say these sentences using the words given.*

1. Everyone in the family comes to my parents' home on Thanksgiving. (gets together)

   Everyone in the family gets together at my parents' home on Thanksgiving.

2. Many people have parties on New Year's Eve. (New Year's Eve/when)

   _____

3. Everyone gives and receives presents on Christmas. (exchange)

   _____

4. After they leave the reception, many couples put on everyday clothes. (change into)

   _____

5. The couple usually leaves the reception before the guests do. (bride and groom)

   _____

10   *Imagine you are in a foreign country and someone has invited you to a New Year's Eve party. Ask questions about the party using the words given in the list or your own ideas.*

☑ present	☐ special food or drink	☐ clothes
☐ flowers	☐ sing and dance	☐ fireworks

1. *Should I bring a New Year's present?* _____

2. _____

3. _____

4. _____

5. _____

6. _____

Back to the future

1 Complete this passage with verbs from the list. Use the past, present, or future tense.

| ☐ buy | ☐ get | ☐ have to | ☐ sell | ☐ use |
| ☐ drive | ☑ go | ☐ make | ☐ have | |

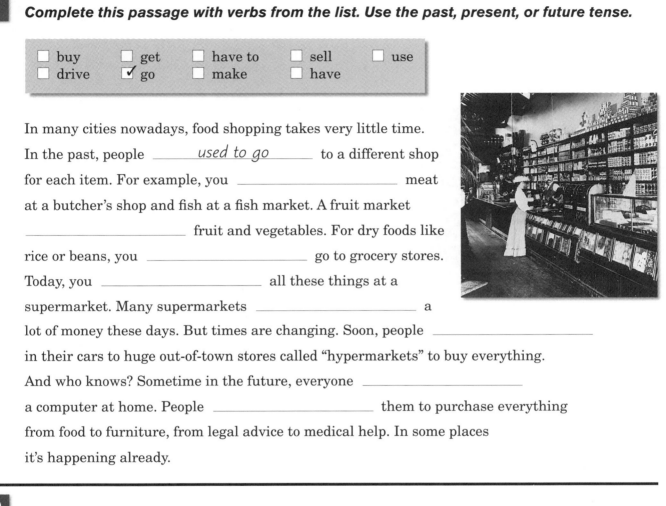

In many cities nowadays, food shopping takes very little time.
In the past, people _____*used to go*_____ to a different shop
for each item. For example, you _____ meat
at a butcher's shop and fish at a fish market. A fruit market
_____ fruit and vegetables. For dry foods like
rice or beans, you _____ go to grocery stores.
Today, you _____ all these things at a
supermarket. Many supermarkets _____ a
lot of money these days. But times are changing. Soon, people _____
in their cars to huge out-of-town stores called "hypermarkets" to buy everything.
And who knows? Sometime in the future, everyone _____
a computer at home. People _____ them to purchase everything
from food to furniture, from legal advice to medical help. In some places
it's happening already.

2 Choose the correct responses.

1. A: When did people travel by horse and carriage?

   B: _____
   ■ Soon.   ■ About 100 years ago.   ■ These days.

2. A: When might doctors find a cure for the flu?

   B: _____
   ■ Nowadays.   ■ In the next 50 years.   ■ A few years ago.

3. A: When did the first man go to the moon?

   B: _____
   ■ Sometime in the future.   ■ Today.   ■ About 30 years ago.

4. A: When are most people going to have computers at home?

   B: _____
   ■ In the past.   ■ Right now.   ■ In the next few years.

3 *Complete the sentences. Use the words given and ideas from the pictures.*

1. These days, *people go to the beach on vacation.* (beach)

   In the future, *they might go to Mars on vacation.* (Mars)

1 Beach Vacation SUN & FUN
Vacation ON MARS and Join the STARS

2

2. In the past, _____ _____ (collect records)

   Nowadays, _____ _____ (collect CDs)

3

3. A few years ago, _____ _____ (typewriters)

   Today, _____ _____ (computers)

4

4. About a hundred years ago, _____ _____ (long dresses)

   These days, _____ _____ (short skirts)

5

Apartments for rent
in new
20-floor building.
Call 555-6724
for information.

Apartments for rent
in new 200-floor
building.
Call 555-0925
for information.

5. Nowadays, _____ _____ (20 floors)

   Sometime in the future, _____ _____ (200 floors)

4 *New forms of energy*

A What forms of energy do you use in your home? Do you think this will change in the next twenty years?

B Read the article.

THE FUTURE OF ENERGY

windmills

E nergy is very important in modern life. People use energy to run machines, heat and cool their homes, cook, give light, and transport people and products from place to place. Most energy nowadays comes from fossil fuels – petroleum, coal, and natural gas. However, burning fossil fuels causes pollution. Also, if we don't find new kinds of energy, we will use up all the fossil fuels in the twenty-first century. Scientists are working to find other kinds of energy for the future. What might these sources of energy be?

Energy from the wind All over the world, people use the power of the wind. It turns windmills and moves sailboats. It is a clean source of energy, and there is lots of it. Unfortunately, if the wind does not blow, there is no wind energy.

Energy from water When water moves from a high place to a lower place, it makes energy. This energy is used to create electricity. In Brittany, France, for example, waterpower produces enough energy to light a town of 40,000 people. Waterpower gives energy without pollution. However, people have to build dams to use this energy. Dams cost a lot of money, so water energy is expensive.

Energy from the earth There is heat in rocks under the earth. Scientists use this heat to make geothermal energy. San Francisco gets half of the energy it needs from geothermal power. This kind of energy is cheap, but it is possible only in a few places in the world.

Energy from the sun Solar panels on the roofs of houses can turn energy from the sun into electricity. These panels can create enough energy to heat an entire house. Solar power is clean and there is a lot of it in sunny places. But when the weather is bad, there is no sunlight for energy.

C What is one advantage and one disadvantage of each type of energy? Complete the chart.

	Advantage	Disadvantage
wind power	_____	_____
waterpower	_____	_____
geothermal power	_____	_____
solar power	_____	_____

5 *Choose the correct responses.*

1. A: What if I get in shape this summer?

   B: _____

   - You might be able to come rock climbing with me.
   - You won't be able to come rock climbing with me.

2. A: What will happen if I stop smoking?

   B: _____

   - Well, you won't gain weight.
   - Well, you might gain weight.

3. A: What if I get a new job?

   B: _____

   - You won't be able to buy new clothes.
   - You'll be able to buy new clothes.

4. A: What will happen if I don't get a summer job?

   B: _____

   - You may be able to live with a roommate when school starts.
   - You'll have to live with a roommate when school starts.

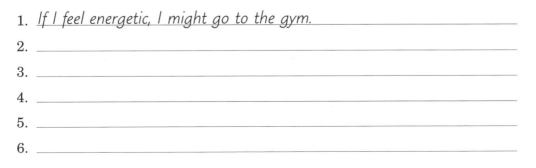

6 *Collocations*

A Which words or phrases go with which verbs? Complete the chart.

☐ a cold	☐ relaxed
☐ dieting	☐ smoking
☑ energetic	☐ touch
☐ married	☐ weight

feel	get	lose	quit
energetic	_____	_____	_____
_____	_____	_____	_____

B Write sentences with *if*. Use some of the words in part A.

1. *If I feel energetic, I might go to the gym.* _____

2. _____

3. _____

4. _____

5. _____

6. _____

7 **Complete these sentences with your own information.**
Add commas where necessary.

> **Grammar note: Conditional sentences with if clauses**
>
> The *if* clause can come before or after the main clause.
>
> **Before the main clause, add a comma:**
> *If I move to a cheaper apartment,* I'll be able to buy a car.
>
> **After the main clause, do not add a comma:**
> I'll be able to buy a car *if I move to a cheaper apartment.*

1. If I go shopping on Saturday, *I might spend too much money.*

2. I'll feel healthier _____

3. If I get more exercise _____

4. If I don't get good grades in school _____

5. I might get more sleep _____

6. I'll be happy _____

---

8 *Nouns and adjectives*

A Complete this chart.

Noun	Adjective	Noun	Adjective
energy	_____	_____	medical
_____	environmental	success	_____
health	_____		

B Complete the sentences. Use words from part A.

1. There have been lots of _____ *medical* _____ advances in the past half century, but there is still no cure for the common cold.

2. There are many _____ problems in my country. There's a lot of air pollution and the oceans are dirty.

3. My _____ is not as good as it used to be. So I've decided to eat better food and go swimming every day.

4. My vacation was a great _____ . I feel much healthier and more relaxed.

5. If I start exercising more often, I might feel more

_____ .

53

9 Rewrite these sentences. Find another way to say each sentence using the words given.

1. If I stop eating rich food, I may be able to lose weight. (diet)

   If I go on a diet, I may be able to lose weight.

2. In the future, not many people will use cash to buy things. (few)

   _____

3. Today, people use bicycles less than before. (used to)

   _____

4. If I get a better job, I can buy an apartment. (be able to)

   _____

5. There's going to be a big new shopping center downtown. (mall)

   _____

10 Write about yourself. In the first paragraph, describe something about your past. In the second paragraph, write about your life now. In the third paragraph, write about your future.

Example:

> I used to live in a very quiet place . . . .
>
> Now, I live in a big city. My job is . . . . If my English improves, I may be able to get a job in an international company . . . .
>
> Next year, I'm going to . . . . I might . . . .

_____

_____

_____

_____

_____

_____

_____

_____

_____

10 I don't like working on weekends!

1 Choose the correct responses.

1. A: I enjoy working in sales.

   B: _____

   - Well, I can. ■ Neither do I. ■ So do I.

2. A: I like working night shifts.

   B: _____

   - Gee, I don't. ■ Neither do I. ■ Neither am I.

3. A: I can't stand getting to work late.

   B: _____

   - I can't. ■ Neither can I. ■ Well, I do.

4. A: I'm interested in using my language skills.

   B: _____

   - So am I. ■ Oh; I don't. ■ Oh, I don't mind.

2 Complete the sentences with words and phrases from the list. Use gerunds.

- ☐ commute
- ☐ learn languages
- ☑ meet deadlines
- ☐ start her own business
- ☐ work on a computer
- ☐ work with a team

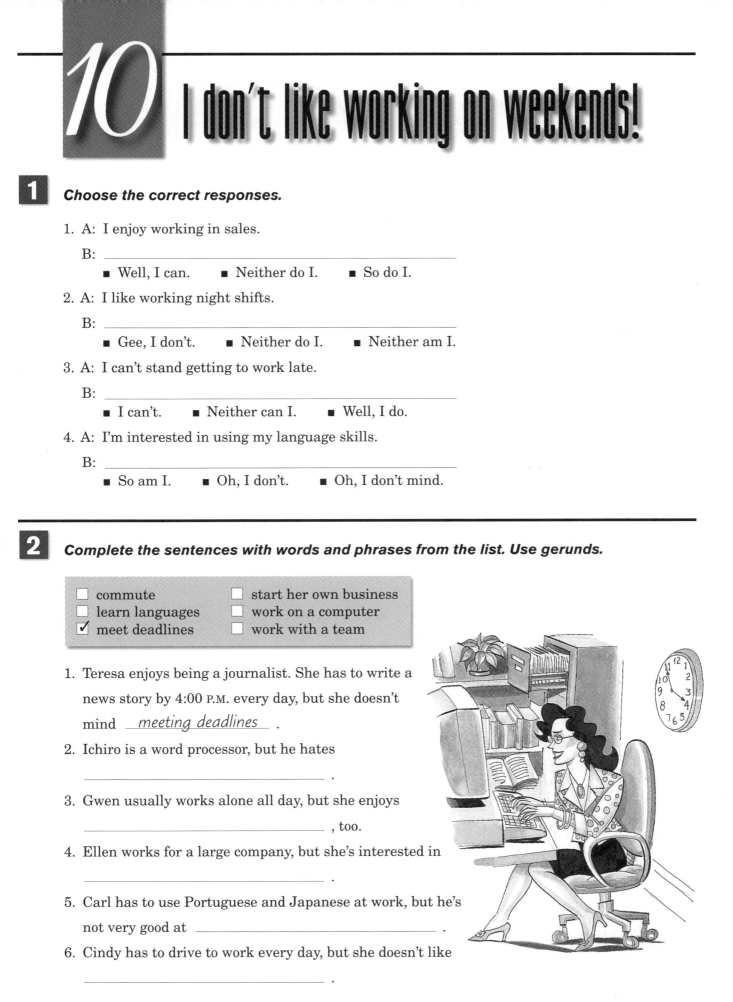

1. Teresa enjoys being a journalist. She has to write a news story by 4:00 P.M. every day, but she doesn't mind _meeting deadlines_ .

2. Ichiro is a word processor, but he hates

   _____ .

3. Gwen usually works alone all day, but she enjoys

   _____ , too.

4. Ellen works for a large company, but she's interested in

   _____ .

5. Carl has to use Portuguese and Japanese at work, but he's not very good at _____ .

6. Cindy has to drive to work every day, but she doesn't like

   _____ .

3 **Rewrite these sentences. Find another way to say each sentence using the words given.**

1. I'm happy to answer the phone. (mind)
   I don't mind answering the phone.

2. I can't make decisions quickly. (not good at)

3. I hate having to meet deadlines. (stand)

4. I don't enjoy working alone. (with a team)

4 **Complete these sentences about yourself. Use gerunds. Add other information if appropriate.**

On the job or at school
1. I like *meeting people, but I'm a little shy.*
2. I can't stand
3. I don't mind

In my free time
4. I'm interested in
5. I'm not interested in

At parties or in social situations
6. I'm good at
7. I'm not very good at

5 **Choose the correct words.**

1. Sam doesn't smile or laugh a lot. He often looks worried about things. He is a very _____ person.
   (serious/strange/strict)

2. You can trust Rose. If she says she's going to do something, she'll do it. She's very _____ .
   (hard-working/level-headed/reliable)

3. Joe isn't good at remembering things. Last week he missed an important business meeting again. He is so _____ .
   (efficient/forgetful/moody)

6 *Jobs on the Internet*

A Have you ever looked for a job on the Internet? What jobs have you seen advertised?

B Read these job ads. Choose a job title from the box for each ad.

☐ flight attendant   ☐ stock broker   ☐ journalist   ☐ truck driver

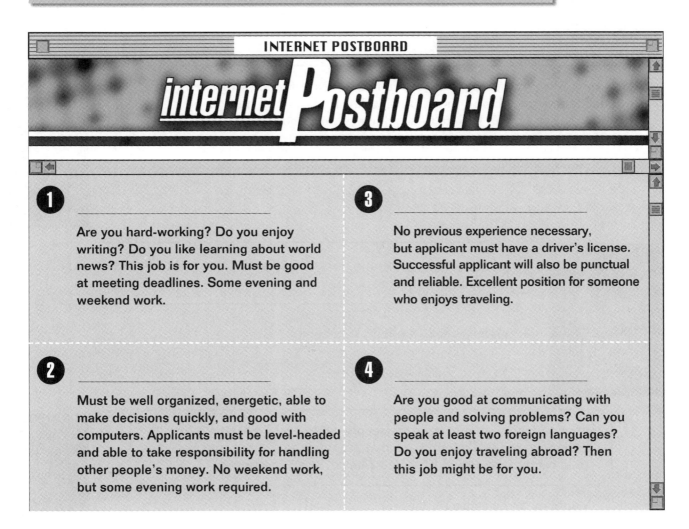

INTERNET POSTBOARD

internet Postboard

1
_____
Are you hard-working? Do you enjoy writing? Do you like learning about world news? This job is for you. Must be good at meeting deadlines. Some evening and weekend work.

2
_____
Must be well organized, energetic, able to make decisions quickly, and good with computers. Applicants must be level-headed and able to take responsibility for handling other people's money. No weekend work, but some evening work required.

3
_____
No previous experience necessary, but applicant must have a driver's license. Successful applicant will also be punctual and reliable. Excellent position for someone who enjoys traveling.

4
_____
Are you good at communicating with people and solving problems? Can you speak at least two foreign languages? Do you enjoy traveling abroad? Then this job might be for you.

C Which would be the best job for you? the worst? Number the jobs from 1 (the best) to 4 (the worst). Give reasons. List your special experience, preferences, or personal traits.

Job	Reason
_____ flight attendant	_____
_____ stock broker	_____
_____ journalist	_____
_____ truck driver	_____

7 *Read what these people say about themselves. Which job should they do? Which job should they avoid? Write two sentences, giving reasons for your answers. Use the phrases given and **because**.*

Jim

> I enjoy helping people, but I can't stand working nights and weekends. I want to be a nurse or a social worker.

1. (make a good/could never) *Jim would make a good social worker because he enjoys helping people. He could never be a nurse because he can't stand working nights and weekends.*

> I really like doing things with my hands. I also enjoy working with wood. I don't enjoy working in the same place every day, and I hate being in noisy places. I think I'd like to be a factory worker or a carpenter.

Anita

2. (could/couldn't) _____

_____

_____

Jill

> I'm good at explaining things and I really like children. I can't stand working long hours. I think I'd like to be a doctor or a teacher.

3. (make a good/would make a bad) _____

_____

_____

> I'm really interested in meeting people, and I enjoy wearing different clothes every day. I'm not so good at organizing my time, and I can't stand computers. I might become a model or an accountant.

Maria

4. (would make a good/could never) _____

_____

_____

Larry

> I'm really good at selling things. I also love helping people. But I'm not so good at solving problems. I think I'd like to be a salesperson or a detective.

5. (could be/wouldn't make a good) _____

_____

_____

8 *Add* a *or* an *in the correct places.*

1. Jerry could never be a nurse or teacher because he is very bad-tempered and impatient with people. On the other hand, he's efficient and reliable person. So he would make good bookkeeper or accountant.

2. Christine would make terrible lawyer or executive. She isn't good at making decisions. On the other hand, she'd make excellent actress or artist because she's very creative and funny.

9 *Opposites*

A Write the opposites. Use the words in the box.

☐ boring	☐ forgetful	☐ lazy	☐ outgoing
☑ disorganized	☐ impatient	☐ moody	☐ unfriendly

1. efficient/ *disorganized*
2. friendly/
3. hard-working/
4. interesting/

5. level-headed/
6. patient/
7. quiet/
8. reliable/

B Complete the sentences with words from part A.

1. Su Yin is a very _____ person. She really enjoys meeting new people.
2. I can't stand working with _____ people. I like having reliable co-workers.
3. Becky is very _____ . One day she's happy and the next day she's sad.
4. Philip is an _____ person. I'm never bored when I talk to him.

10 **Use these words to complete the crossword puzzle.**

☐ creative   ☐ efficient   ☐ impatient   ☐ reliable   ☐ tempered
☐ critical   ☐ forgetful   ☐ level   ☐ strange   ☐ working
☑ disorganized   ☐ generous   ☐ punctual   ☐ strict

Across

1 Amy should not be an accountant because she's very _____ . She can never find the information she needs.

5 I always do good work and meet my deadlines. My boss never has to worry because I'm _____ .

6 Ed would make a great nurse because he's so _____-headed. He never gets anxious when things go wrong.

7 Jack writes great children's stories. He's very _____ and always thinks of new ideas.

11 A good lawyer has to remember facts. Jerry is a terrible lawyer because he's very _____ .

12 My favorite teacher at school was Mrs. Matthews. She was pretty _____ , but we had a lot of fun, too.

13 Laura is very hard-_____ . She works ten hours a day, six days a week.

Down

2 Dawn is a terrible social worker because she's very _____ . She can't stand waiting for other people.

3 My mother was very _____ . She gave me $500 for my birthday.

4 Sam is very bad-_____ and moody. He gets angry at unimportant things.

8 June's secretary is very _____ . She types twice as fast as most secretaries, and she never wastes time.

9 I can't stand my boss. She complains about everything I do. She's so _____ .

10 Larry arrives on time every day, even when there's a terrible traffic jam. He's always _____ .

12 Martha is very _____ . She does odd things. She often gets up in the middle of the night and does her chores.

It's really worth seeing!

1 *Complete these sentences. Use the passive form of the verbs in the list.*

☐ compose	☐ discover	☐ paint
☑ design	☐ invent	☐ write

1. The Bank of China building in Hong Kong
   _____*was designed*_____ by the architect
   I. M. Pei in the 1980s.

2. The play *Romeo and Juliet* _____
   by William Shakespeare in the 1590s.

3. The telephone _____ by Alexander
   Graham Bell in 1876.

4. The picture *Sunflowers* _____ by
   Vincent van Gogh in 1888.

5. Penicillin _____ by
   Sir Alexander Fleming in 1929.

6. The music for the film *West Side Story*
   _____ by Leonard Bernstein in 1957.

the Bank of China building

2 *Change these active sentences into the passive.*

1. Agatha Christie wrote many famous mysteries.
   Many famous mysteries were written by Agatha Christie.

2. Mary Shelley wrote the novel *Frankenstein*.

   _____

3. Frank Lloyd Wright designed the Guggenheim Museum in New York City.

   _____

4. The Soviet Union launched the first space satellite in 1957.

   _____

5. Dr. Christiaan Barnard performed the first human heart transplant in 1967.

   _____

3 *Write sentences about each landmark. Use the passive.*

1 **Big Ben**

builder: Sir Benjamin Hall
date: 1859

2 **the Eiffel Tower**

designer: Gustave Eiffel
date: 1889

3 **the pyramids**

builders: the ancient Egyptians
date: about 2500 B.C.

4 **the Sydney Opera House**

designer: Jorn Utzon   date: 1973

5 **Brasília**

planners: Lucio Costa and Oscar Niemeyer
date: the late 1950s

1. <u>*Big Ben was built by Sir Benjamin Hall in 1859.*</u>
2. _____
3. _____
4. _____
5. _____

4 Which capital city?

A Read about these capital cities. Match the cities in the list with the correct descriptions below.

- ☐ London, England
- ☐ Mexico City, Mexico
- ☐ Madrid, Spain
- ☐ Ottawa, Canada
- ☐ Manila, the Philippines
- ☐ Rome, Italy

_____ According to many historians, this city was founded in 753 B.C. by Romulus and was named after him. However, the name may come from Ruma, the old name for the Tiber River.

_____ This city was founded by the Spanish on an island in a lake. Both the country and the city are named after an older name for the city, *Metz-xih-co*, which means "in the center of the waters of the moon."

_____ This city was made the capital in 1561. Its name may come from the Arabic name Medshrid, meaning "timber." Good supplies of timber were found in the area at the time.

_____ The Romans founded this city in the first century B.C. In Roman times, it was known as Londinium, which may have been the name of a group of people.

_____ Founded in 1571, this city takes its name from Tagalog, a language that is widely spoken there. It means "a place where the plant indigo is found" (*may* = "there is"; *nila* = "indigo").

_____ This city became the capital of the country in the middle of the nineteenth century. Its name is taken from the word *Adawa* in the Algonquin Indian language, which probably means "to trade."

Ottawa, Canada

Rome, Italy

B Check (✓) True or False. For statements that are false, write the true information.

	True	False
1. Rome was named after a person or a mountain.	☐	☐
2. Madrid and Manila were named after products that were found there.	☐	☐
3. Ottawa was named after the activities of the Indians in that region.	☐	☐
4. London and Mexico City were given names about their location.	☐	☐

5 *Add* is *or* are *where necessary.*

Ecuador ^{is} situated on the equator in the northwest of South America. It made up of a coastal plain in the west and a tropical rain forest in the east. These two areas separated by the Andes mountains in the center of the country.

The economy based on oil and agricultural products. More oil produced in Ecuador than any other South American country except Venezuela. Bananas, coffee, and cocoa grown there. Many of these products exported. Hardwood also produced and exported.

The people are mostly of Indian origin. Several Indian languages spoken there, for example, Quechua. Spanish spoken in Ecuador, too. The currency called the sucre.

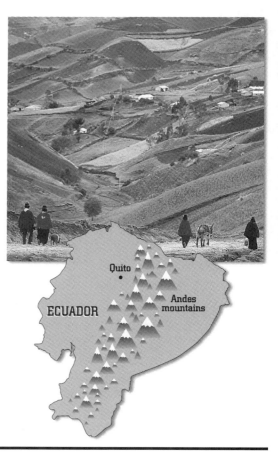

6 *Complete the sentences. Use words from the list.*

☑ agricultural	☐ electronics	☐ peso	☐ wheat
☐ beef	☐ mining	☐ tourism	

1. France exports _____*agricultural*_____ products such as milk, butter, and cheese.

2. The _____ is the currency that is used in Chile.

3. _____ is a very important industry in Italy. Millions of people visit every year.

4. Gold _____ is an important industry in South Africa.

5. Much of the world's _____ is grown in the Canadian prairies. It's used to make foods like bread and pasta.

6. A lot of meat, especially _____ , is exported from Argentina.

7. The _____ industry was developed in many Asian countries in the 1980s. Now, a lot of computers and televisions are exported from countries like South Korea.

7 **Complete this paragraph with is or are and the past participle of the verbs in the list. You will use some of the verbs more than once.**

call	fill	know	produce	visit
divide	find	locate	surround	

*E*very year, millions of tourists visit California. California ___*is known*___ for its beautiful scenery, warm climate, and excellent food. There are twenty national parks in California. They _____ by over thirty million people every year. Many world-famous museums _____ there, including the Getty Museum in Malibu and the San Francisco Museum of Modern Art.

The state _____ into two parts, called Northern California and Southern California. San Francisco and Yosemite National Park _____ in Northern California. San Francisco _____ by water on three sides and is a city with a beautiful bay and several bridges. Its streets _____ always _____ with tourists. On the north end of the bay is Napa Valley, where many excellent wines _____ . South of San Francisco, there is an area that is famous for its computer industries; it _____ Silicon Valley. Many computer industries _____ there. Los Angeles, Hollywood, and Disneyland _____ in Southern California. Southern California _____ for its desert areas, which are sometimes next to snowcapped mountains. Southern California is one of the few places in the world where you can ski in the morning and surf in the afternoon.

8 **Rewrite these sentences. Find another way to say each sentence using the words given.**

1. Sir Paul McCartney wrote the song *Mull of Kintyre*. (written)

   _____

2. I. M. Pei designed the new entrance to the Louvre in Paris. (by)

   _____

3. They speak German, French, and Italian in Switzerland. (spoken)

   _____

4. Malaysia has a prime minister. (governed)

   _____

9 Wh-questions and indirect questions

A Look at the answers. Write Wh-questions.

1. Who _____
   The Color Purple was written by Alice Walker.

2. What _____
   Rice is produced in Thailand.

3. Where _____
   Acapulco is located in Mexico.

4. When _____
   Santiago, Chile, was founded in 1541.

B Look at the answers. Write indirect questions.

1. Do you know _____
   The Golden Gate Bridge was completed in 1937.

2. Can you tell me _____
   Don Quixote was written by Miguel de Cervantes.

3. Do you know _____
   Antibiotics were first used in 1941.

4. Could you tell me _____
   The tea bag was invented by Joseph Kreiger in 1920.

10 Complete the sentences. Use the passive of the words given.

1804 The first steam locomotive _____was built_____ (build) in Britain.

1829 A speed record of 35 mph (48 kph) _____
     (establish) by a train in Britain.

1857 Steel rails _____ (use) for the first time in Britain.

1863 The world's first underground railway _____
     (open) in London.

1869 The air brake _____ (develop) by the
     U.S. inventor George Westinghouse. This made high-speed train
     travel possible.

1898 The first U.S. subway system _____ (open) in Boston.

1964 "Bullet train" service _____ (introduce) in Japan.

1990 A speed of 320 mph (512 kph) _____ (reach) by the
     French high-speed train (called "TGV").

1995 Maglevs _____ (test) in several countries. These trains
     use magnets to lift them above the ground.

early steam locomotive

12 It's been a long time!

1 *A fire alarm went off in an apartment building last night. Describe what these people were doing then. Use the past continuous.*

1 Kathy and David
2 Mr. Yuen
3 the Hardings
5 Andrew
6 Ann
4 Jenny

1. *Kathy and David were playing chess.*
2. _____
3. _____
4. _____
5. _____
6. _____

2 *Describe your activities yesterday. Where were you, and what were you doing?*

1. At 9:00 A.M., *I was with friends. We were having breakfast at a coffee shop before class.*

2. At 11:00 in the morning, _____

_____

3. At noon, _____

_____

4. In the afternoon, _____

_____

5. At 10:00 last night, _____

_____

6. At this time yesterday, _____

_____

3 **Complete the conversation with the correct words or phrases.**

Carl: How did you get your first job, Anita?

Anita: Well, I _____*got*_____ a summer job in a department store
           (got/was getting)

      while I _____ at the university.
          (studied/was studying)

Carl: No, I mean your first *full-time* job.

Anita: But that is how I got my first full-time job. I _____ during the
                         (worked/was working)

      summer when the manager _____ me a job
                  (offered/was offering)

      after graduation.

Carl: Wow. That's lucky. Did you like the job?

Anita: Well, I did at first, but then things changed. I _____ the same
                    (did/was doing)

      thing every day, but they _____ me any responsibility.
                (didn't give/weren't giving)

      I _____ really bored when another company
        (got/was getting)

      _____ me to work for them.
      (asked/was asking)

---

4 **Look at the pictures and complete these sentences.**

1. I was having lots of problems with my
boyfriend when *he asked me to marry him.*

2. I met a really nice guy last week while ____
_____

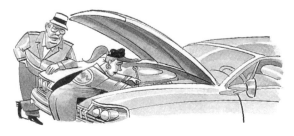

3. My car was giving me a lot of trouble, so
_____

4. Dinner arrived while _____
_____

5 Work hard, play hard

A What do you know about Bill Gates?

B Read the article.

Bill Gates III is a very important person in the computer industry. He has been chief executive officer of Microsoft Corporation for several years. He is also the richest person in the United States. How did he do it?

He learned a lot from his parents. While Bill was going to school, his father went to college, got a degree, and became a successful lawyer. From this, Bill learned that you have to work hard if you want something. His mother was a very busy teacher, but she also enjoyed going to parties. From this, he learned something else: If you want to work hard *and* play hard, you have to make a schedule.

When Bill was young, he spent a lot of time alone. While most of his friends were playing, Bill read all of the *World Book Encyclopedia* and finished it when he was 8 years old.

Bill's childhood was not all work, however. He used to play a lot of sports – swimming, water-skiing, tennis. He was very serious about sports. He loved winning and he hated losing. When Bill got older, he spent more and more time working – and playing – on a computer.

Before he was 20, Bill developed the world's first computer language for the personal computer. Once when he was thinking about the future, he realized something important. He thought that every home was going to have a computer, and every computer would need software – his software. He said, "I'm going to make my first million dollars on software by the time I'm 25." And he did!

C Check (✓) True or False. For statements that are false, write the true information.

	True	False
1. Bill Gates learned that you have to play hard for what you want.	☐	☐
2. He used to read a lot when he was young.	☐	☐
3. He was happy to lose a game of tennis.	☐	☐
4. He enjoyed playing games on the computer.	☐	☐
5. He wasn't making much money when he was 25 years old.	☐	☐

6 How long has it been?

A Write sentences. Use the present perfect continuous and *for* or *since*.

> **Grammar note: for *and* since**
>
> **Use *for* to describe a period of time in the past.**
> Linda has been living in Seattle **for three months.**
> I haven't been working there **for very long.**
>
> **Use *since* to describe a point of time in the past.**
> Linda has been living in Seattle **since she changed jobs.**
> I haven't been working there **since last summer.**

1. Jessica/work/model/3 years
   Jessica has been working as a model for three years.

2. Ruth and Peter/go/graduate school/August

3. Jim/study/Chinese/a year

4. Maria/not teach/she had a baby

5. Cindy/not live/Los Angeles/very long

6. Felix and Anna/travel/South America/six weeks

B Write sentences about yourself. Use the phrases and clauses in the list or phrases and clauses of your own, and *for* or *since*.

I was a child	I was in high school
eighteen months	1996
a few weeks	ages

1. *I've been interested in movies since I was a child.*
2.
3.
4.
5.
6.

7 Look at the answers. Write the questions.

Chris: _What have you been doing lately?_

Alex: I've been working a lot and trying to stay in shape.

Chris: _____

Alex: No, I haven't been jogging. I've been playing tennis in the evenings with friends.

Chris: Really? _____

Alex: No, I've been losing most of the games. But it's fun. How about you?

_____

Chris: No, I haven't been getting any exercise. I've been working long hours.

Alex: _____

Chris: Yes, I've been working weekends. I've been working Saturday mornings.

Alex: Well, why don't we play a game of tennis on Saturday afternoon? It's great exercise!

8 Choose the correct responses.

1. A: When I was a kid, I lived in New Zealand.

   B: _____
   - Wow! Tell me more.
   - Oh, have you?
   - So have I.

2. A: I haven't been ice-skating for ages.

   B: _____
   - Why were you?
   - Wow! I have, too.
   - Neither have I.

3. A: I was a teenager when I got my first job.

   B: _____
   - Really? Where do you work?
   - Really? That's interesting.
   - For five years.

4. A: I haven't seen you for a long time.

   B: _____
   - In five years.
   - Not since we graduated.
   - Gee, I have no idea.

9 **Complete the answers to the questions. Use the past continuous or the present perfect continuous of the verbs given.**

1. A: Have you been working here for long?

    B: No, I _____*haven't been working*_____ (work) here for very long –
    only since January.

2. A: Were you living in Europe before you moved here?

    B: No, I _____ (live) in Korea.

3. A: How long have you been studying English?

    B: I _____ (study) it for about a year.

4. A: What were you doing before you went back to school?

    B: I _____ (sell) real estate.

5. A: What have you been doing since I last saw you?

    B: I _____ (travel) around Europe.

10 **Rewrite these sentences. Find another way to say each sentence using the words given.**

1. I was getting dressed when my date arrived. (while)

    While I was getting dressed, my date arrived.

2. He was about 15 when he started saving up for a world trip. (adolescent)

    _____

    _____

3. I was commuting to work when I lived out of town. (suburbs)

    _____

    _____

4. I've had a part-time job since last year. (a year)

    _____

    _____

5. I've been spending too much money lately. (not save enough)

    _____

    _____

6. I haven't seen you for a long time. (ages)

    _____

    _____

13 A terrific book, but a terrible movie!

1 *Choose the correct words to complete these movie reviews.*

★ ★ ★ ★ *Today's* MOVIE Reviews

The President

Nathan Kane's movie *The President* is based on a true story about the life of a president. But don't watch this movie if you're ___*interested*___ in
(interested/interesting)
history. It isn't all true. However, Kane makes the film
_____ , and the editing is outstanding.
(excited/exciting)
I was also _____ by the photography,
(amazed/amazing)
which certainly deserves to win an Oscar.

The Patient

You will be _____ at how good *The*
(surprised/surprising)
Patient is. It is one of the most _____
(fascinated/fascinating)
films I've ever seen. It's a romantic story about four
people during the Second World War. All the actors
are fantastic. You won't be _____ for
(bored/boring)
one second. A must-see.

2 *Choose the correct words.*

1. *Independence Day* was a ___*marvelous*___
   (absurd/disgusting/marvelous) movie, and
   I'd love to see it a second time.

2. I think Spielberg's movie *The Lost World*
   is as good as *Jurassic Park*. In fact, it's really
   _____ (terrible/terrific/boring).

3. The dogs were really great in *101 Dalmations*.
   I don't know how they made them do
   such _____ (dreadful/dumb/
   fantastic) things.

4. Uma Thurman is _____
   (horrible/ridiculous/wonderful) in *Pulp Fiction*.
   I think she's a really great actress.

a scene from the movie *Independence Day*

3 *Choose the correct responses.*

1. A: I think that Tom Cruise is very
   good-looking.

   B: *Oh, I do, too.*
   - Oh, I do, too.
   - I don't like him, either.

2. A: His new movie is the dumbest
   movie I've ever seen.

   B: _____
   - Yeah, I liked it, too.
   - I didn't like it, either.

3. A: It's weird that they don't show movie
   classics on TV. I really like them.

   B: _____
   - I know. It's really wonderful.
   - I know. It's strange.

4. A: I think Glenn Close is an
   outstanding actress.

   B: _____
   - Yeah, she's horrible.
   - Yeah, she's excellent.

5. A: The movie we saw last night
   was ridiculous.

   B: _____
   - Yes, I agree. It was exciting.
   - Well, I thought it was pretty good.

4 *Write two sentences for each of these categories.*

1. Things you think are exciting
   I think water-skiing is exciting.
   _____

2. Things you are interested in
   _____
   _____

3. Things you think are boring
   _____
   _____

4. Things you are disgusted by
   _____
   _____

5 *Classics on video*

A What are your two favorite classic movies? Why do you like them?

B Read about these videos for rent. Match the kind of movie with the correct video description.

_____ a horror film   _____ a romance   _____ a musical   _____ a science fiction film

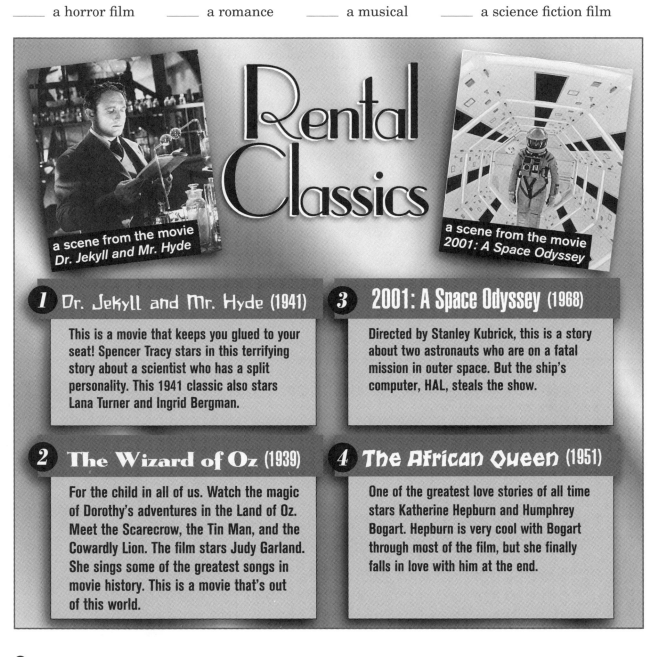

Rental Classics

a scene from the movie
Dr. Jekyll and Mr. Hyde

a scene from the movie
2001: A Space Odyssey

1 Dr. Jekyll and Mr. Hyde (1941)

This is a movie that keeps you glued to your seat! Spencer Tracy stars in this terrifying story about a scientist who has a split personality. This 1941 classic also stars Lana Turner and Ingrid Bergman.

2 The Wizard of Oz (1939)

For the child in all of us. Watch the magic of Dorothy's adventures in the Land of Oz. Meet the Scarecrow, the Tin Man, and the Cowardly Lion. The film stars Judy Garland. She sings some of the greatest songs in movie history. This is a movie that's out of this world.

3 2001: A Space Odyssey (1968)

Directed by Stanley Kubrick, this is a story about two astronauts who are on a fatal mission in outer space. But the ship's computer, HAL, steals the show.

4 The African Queen (1951)

One of the greatest love stories of all time stars Katherine Hepburn and Humphrey Bogart. Hepburn is very cool with Bogart through most of the film, but she finally falls in love with him at the end.

C Write the name of the movie described.

1. a story about two people who fall in love: _____

2. a good movie for children to see: _____

3. so interesting you can't stop watching it: _____

4. has a fascinating character who is loved by the audience: _____

6   *Tell me more!*

A   Rewrite these sentences. Use *who* or *which*.

1. *Star Wars* is a movie that has been very successful for a long time.
   <u>*Star Wars* is a movie which has been very successful for a long time.</u>

2. *Shine* is a movie that is based on a true story about an Australian pianist.

   _____

3. Geoffrey Rush is the actor that won an award for his role in the movie *Shine*.

   _____

4. Mae West is an actress that was known for her roles in silent films.

   _____

5. *The Last Emperor* is a great movie that won a lot of awards.

   _____

6. Ginger Rogers was an actress and dancer that made a lot of films about fifty years ago.

   _____

B   Write two sentences like those in part A about movies or entertainers. Use *who* or *which*.

1. _____

2. _____

7   *Complete the sentences. Use* that *for things and* who *for people.*

Karen: Which one is Keanu Reeves?

Pedro: Oh, you know him. He's the one ___who___ starred in *Speed*.

Karen: Yeah, I remember. That's one movie _____ was really exciting. We were glued to our seats.

Pedro: Right. Reeves is a detective _____ is hunted by a crazy guy. The guy puts a bomb on a bus _____ has a lot of people on it.

Karen: What happens to the people? I forgot.

Pedro: Well, a woman _____ is on the bus gets really frightened and . . .

Karen: Oh, now I remember: there's the bus _____ can't stop, the girl _____ gets hurt, the man _____ gets caught, and the couple _____ fall in love.

Pedro: Yeah! What a great movie!

a scene from the movie *Speed*

8 *Different kinds of movies*

A Write definitions for these different kinds of movies. Use relative clauses and the phrases in the box.

- [ ] has cowboys in it
- [ ] is scary
- [✓] has lots of excitement
- [ ] has songs
- [ ] makes you laugh
- [ ] tells you about animals or plants
- [ ] has a love story

1. An action movie *is a movie that has lots of excitement.*

2. A romance _____

3. A comedy _____

4. A western _____

5. A horror film _____

6. A musical _____

7. A nature film _____

B What kind of movie in part A is your favorite? your least favorite? Write about each one and give reasons for your opinions.

My Favorite Kind of Movie

Example: *I really like action movies. They are movies that make me forget about all my problems.*

_____

_____

_____

_____

My Least Favorite Kind of Movie

Example: *I don't like horror movies because I think they are really dumb. Usually, the story has characters who are not very scary.*

_____

_____

_____

_____

9 **Complete these sentences. Use words in the box.**

> ☐ character   ☐ special effects
> ☐ composer   ☐ photography

1. I thought the _____ in *Star Wars* were terrific.
   They were well made and exciting to watch.

2. I think the _____ in *Dances with Wolves* is marvelous.
   There are lots of scenes with wild animals in the beautiful American West.

3. Harrison Ford plays the main _____ in
   Raiders of the Lost Ark.

4. I've forgotten the name of the _____ who
   wrote the music for the film *Ransom*.

10 **Rewrite this movie review. Where possible, join sentences with *who, that,* or *which*.**

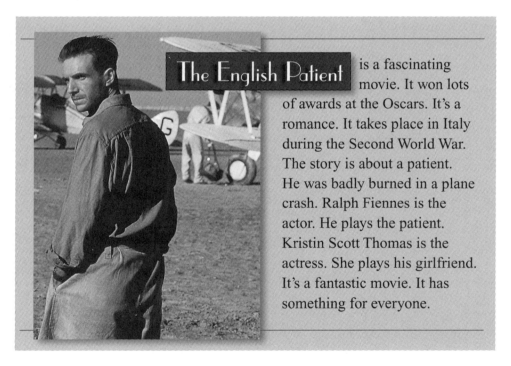

The English Patient is a fascinating movie. It won lots of awards at the Oscars. It's a romance. It takes place in Italy during the Second World War. The story is about a patient. He was badly burned in a plane crash. Ralph Fiennes is the actor. He plays the patient. Kristin Scott Thomas is the actress. She plays his girlfriend. It's a fantastic movie. It has something for everyone.

The English Patient is a fascinating movie that won lots of awards
at the Oscars. . . .

_____

_____

_____

_____

14 So that's what it means!

1 What does that mean?

A What do these gestures mean? Match the phrases in the box with the gestures.

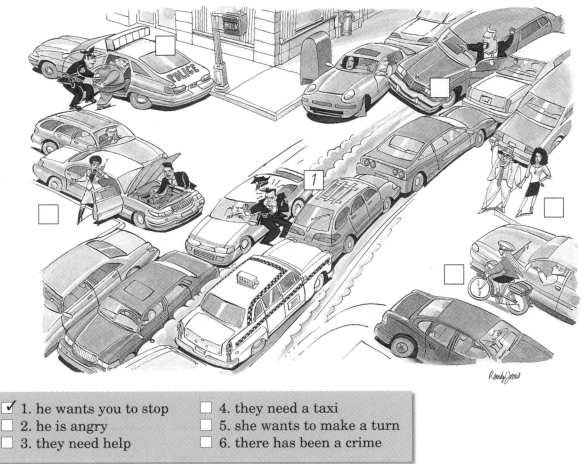

☑ 1. he wants you to stop	☐ 4. they need a taxi
☐ 2. he is angry	☐ 5. she wants to make a turn
☐ 3. they need help	☐ 6. there has been a crime

B Write a sentence about each situation in part A using these phrases:

It could mean . . .	It might mean . . .	It must mean . . .
Maybe it means . . .	Perhaps it means . . .	It probably means . . .

1. *It probably means he wants you to stop.* _____
2. _____
3. _____
4. _____
5. _____
6. _____

2 Emotions

A Do these words describe positive or negative emotions?
Write **P** or **N** next to each word.

annoyed __N__   disgusted _____   excited _____   interested _____

confused _____   embarrassed _____   frightened _____   shocked _____

B Complete the sentences. Choose the correct form of the words in the box.

☐ amazed/amazing   ☑ embarrassed/embarrassing   ☐ frightened/frightening
☐ disgusted/disgusting   ☐ confused/confusing

1. I couldn't get into the parking space and everyone was
   looking at me. I was so _____*embarrassed*_____ .

2. That sign is really _____ .
   What does it mean? It's not clear at all.

3. I'm _____ . I passed
   my test, and I didn't even study for it.

4. The food in that restaurant on the highway is
   _____ . I'll never eat there again!

5. The new horror movie is pretty scary. Some of the
   scenes are really _____ .

3 What would you say in each situation? Use the sentences in the box.

☐ I'm scared.   ☐ That sounds crazy.   ☑ I give up.   ☐ Pay attention.

1. You're losing a game of chess.
   I give up.

2. You want to show your kids how to build a tree house.
   _____

3. A friend asks you to go to a horror movie but you don't like horror films.
   _____

4. Your friend wishes he had green hair and orange eyes.
   _____

4 *Proverbs*

A Match the proverbs with their meanings.

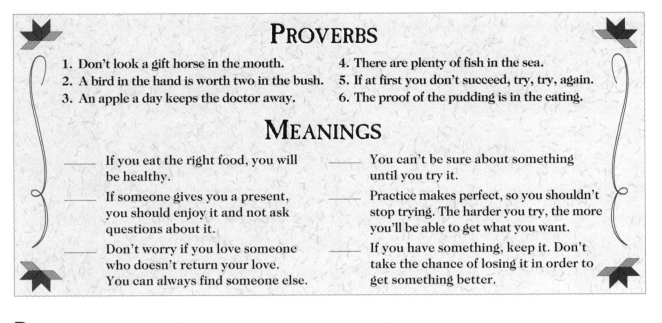

PROVERBS

1. Don't look a gift horse in the mouth.
2. A bird in the hand is worth two in the bush.
3. An apple a day keeps the doctor away.
4. There are plenty of fish in the sea.
5. If at first you don't succeed, try, try, again.
6. The proof of the pudding is in the eating.

MEANINGS

_____ If you eat the right food, you will be healthy.

_____ If someone gives you a present, you should enjoy it and not ask questions about it.

_____ Don't worry if you love someone who doesn't return your love. You can always find someone else.

_____ You can't be sure about something until you try it.

_____ Practice makes perfect, so you shouldn't stop trying. The harder you try, the more you'll be able to get what you want.

_____ If you have something, keep it. Don't take the chance of losing it in order to get something better.

B What would you say? Choose a proverb for each situation.

1. A: Oh, yuck. Those fried brains look disgusting.

   B: Try them. They're delicious.

   A: Really? Oh, they are good. I'm shocked.

   B: See. _____

2. A: Hey, what happened? You look so sad.

   B: I am. You know that guy I was dating. Well, last night he said he didn't want to see me anymore.

   A: Well, don't be too worried. You'll find someone else. _____

   _____

   B: Thanks a lot. That really helps!

3. A: You know, the person who sits next to me in class gave me these flowers for my birthday. I'm amazed. I don't even know his name. What does that mean?

   B: _____

   That was really nice. Just say thank you and don't worry.

C What do you think these proverbs mean?

1. Don't cry over spilled milk.

   It could mean _____

2. Don't judge a book by its cover.

   Maybe it means _____

5 Complete the sentences. Use the words and phrases in the box.
Use each word or phrase only once.

- ☐ must
- ☑ have to
- ☐ can
- ☐ can't
- ☐ aren't allowed to
- ☐ are allowed to

1

1. Father: Well, first you ___*have to*___ start the car.

   Son: Oh, yeah. I almost forgot.

2. Father: OK. Now remember,

   you _____

   go above the speed limit.

   Son: I know.

2

MPH
40

3. Son: What does that sign mean?

   Father: That means you

   _____ turn left.

   Son: OK.

3

4. Father: See that sign? It means you

   _____ turn left or

   you _____ go straight.

   Let's turn left, but be careful.

   Son: OK. This is great, Dad. It's easy.

4

5. Father: Hey, stop! Didn't you see that sign? It means you

   _____ come to a complete stop.

   Son: What sign? I don't see any sign.

   Father: That's a problem!

5

6 *Rewrite these sentences. Find another way to say each sentence using the words given.*

1. Maybe it means you're not allowed to fish here. (may)

   _____

2. You can't light a fire here. (allowed)

   _____

3. Perhaps that sign means you're not allowed to swim here. (might)

   _____

4. I think that sign means you can get food here. (probably)

   _____

7 *Complete the conversation. Use each phrase from the list only once.*

Tony: So, tell me what all these signs mean, Kanya.

Kanya: Well, this one is the fan. _____*You can use it*_____ to heat or cool your car.

Tony: And what about this one?

Kanya: That's your horn. You know, in the city, _____ use it after midnight.

Tony: OK. I'll try to remember that. And what does this one mean?

Kanya: I'm not sure. _____ the hazard light. When your car breaks down, you turn it on.

Tony: What's this mean?

Kanya: Oh, that's your fuel light. _____ add gas when the light is on.

Tony: So, how do you like my new car?

Kanya: Like it? I love it! _____ let me drive it.

Tony: Uh, I don't think so.

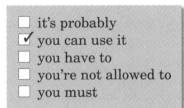

☐ it's probably
☑ you can use it
☐ you have to
☐ you're not allowed to
☐ you must

8 **Complete each conversation using words from the box.**

> ☐ amazing   ☐ annoying   ☐ embarrassing   ☐ shocking

1. A: I fell asleep during class this afternoon. The teacher woke me up.

   B: Oh, that's _____

2. A: I went to the movies last night. The couple who sat behind me talked during the entire movie.

   B: That's _____

3. A: Everyone in my office was just fired.

   B: Oh, that's _____

4. A: You speak English very well.

   B: Thank you. I learned it three months ago.

   A: That's _____

---

9 **Crossword puzzle: Adjectives**

Use these words to complete the crossword puzzle.

> ☐ annoyed   ☐ disgusted   ☑ frightened
> ☐ bored   ☐ excited   ☐ interested
> ☐ confused   ☐ fascinated ☐ worried

Across

1 Someone knocked loudly on my door at 3 A.M. I was really _____ , but I think it was just someone being silly.

4 I'm going to Europe for my vacation. I can't wait to go. I'm so _____ about it.

6 I'm pretty _____ about the test tomorrow. I haven't studied for it, and I know I'm going to fail.

7 I was _____ by all the food in the college cafeteria. It looked so awful that I didn't have any lunch.

8 I'm _____ with this program. Can I turn the TV off?

Down

1 I was really _____ by Joe's vacation photos. He had some beautiful pictures of the Andes mountains in South America.

2 I wasn't _____ in the clothes he was trying to sell me, so I went to another clothes store.

3 I was pretty _____ with Anna when she arrived at my birthday party three hours late.

5 What does that sign mean? I'm completely _____ by it.

15 What would you do?

1 I think I'd . . . .

A What would you do? Check (✓) your answers. If you would do something else, write your suggestion next to "other."

1. A bank truck overturns and millions of dollar bills fall out.
   - ☐ collect the money and keep it
   - ☐ collect the money and return it
   - ☐ other: _____

2. Someone climbs through your neighbor's window.
   - ☐ call the police
   - ☐ ring the doorbell
   - ☐ other: _____

3. Your boss makes things difficult for you at work.
   - ☐ talk to your boss
   - ☐ look for another job
   - ☐ other: _____

4. A friend sounds unhappy on the phone.
   - ☐ ask your friend if he or she has a problem
   - ☐ tell lots of jokes to make your friend laugh
   - ☐ other: _____

B Write about what you would do in the situations in part A. Use phrases from the box.

I'd . . .	I might . . .	I guess . . .
I'd probably . . .	I think I'd . . .	

1. *If a bank truck overturned and millions of dollar bills fell out,*
   I'd probably collect the money and return it.

2. _____
   _____

3. _____
   _____

4. _____
   _____

2 *Complete these sentences with information about yourself.*

1. If a relative asked to borrow some money, I'd _____

2. If I had three wishes, _____

3. If I could have any job I wanted, _____

4. If I had a month to live, _____

5. If I could change one thing about myself, _____

3 *Choose the correct words.*

1. When I went back to the parking lot, I tried to get into someone else's car ____*by*____ mistake.
   (by/in/with)

2. If I saw a friend cheating on an exam, I know exactly what I'd do.
   I'd go _____ to the teacher.
   (actually/probably/straight)

3. I'm in a difficult _____ at work. I don't
   (divorce/predicament/problem)
   know whether to talk to my boss about it or just quit.

4. If I saw someone _____ in a store,
   (disagreeing/shoplifting/shopping)
   I'd tell the store detective immediately.

5. I just won $20,000 in the lottery. I think I'll _____ it.
   (invest/return/sell)

6. I've just read a great novel. Would you like to _____ it?
   (accept/borrow/lose)

7. Tom has a drinking problem, but he _____ it.
   (denies/disagrees/dislikes)
   He says there is nothing wrong.

8. My aunt _____ to lend me her car because
   (agreed/forgot/refused)
   she thinks I'm a terrible driver.

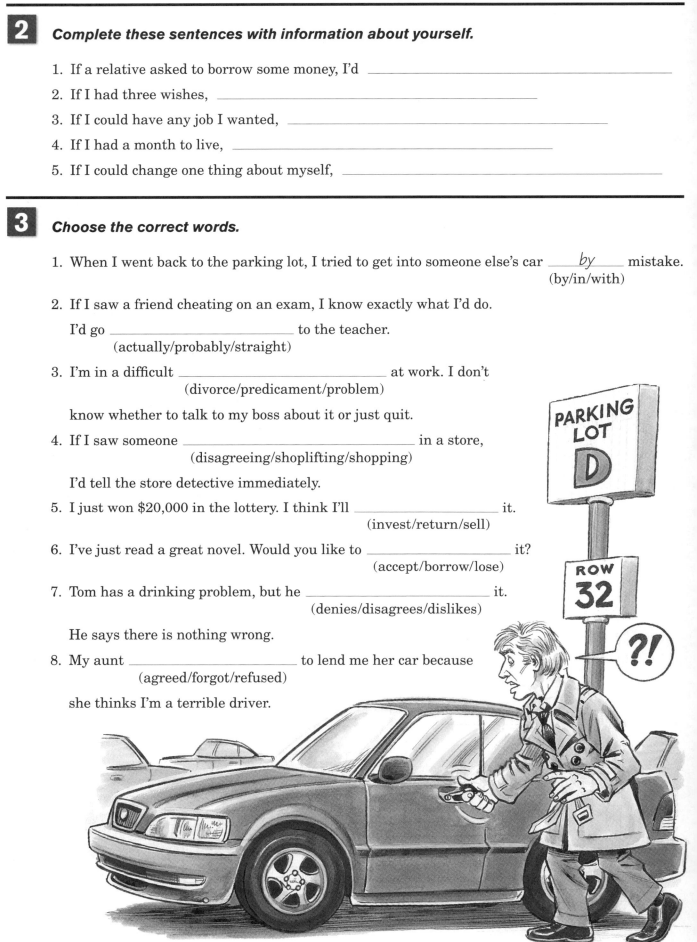

4 Can you advise me?

A If you have a problem, do you usually try to solve it yourself, or do you ask your friends for advice?

B Match these problems with the advice below.

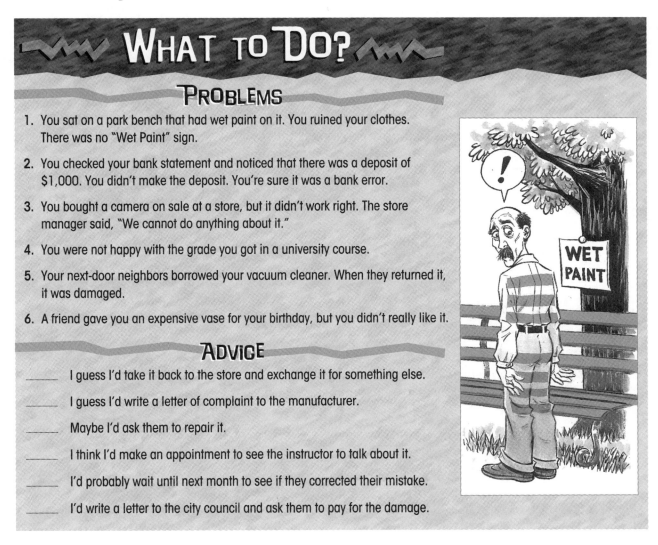

WHAT TO DO?

PROBLEMS

1. You sat on a park bench that had wet paint on it. You ruined your clothes. There was no "Wet Paint" sign.

2. You checked your bank statement and noticed that there was a deposit of $1,000. You didn't make the deposit. You're sure it was a bank error.

3. You bought a camera on sale at a store, but it didn't work right. The store manager said, "We cannot do anything about it."

4. You were not happy with the grade you got in a university course.

5. Your next-door neighbors borrowed your vacuum cleaner. When they returned it, it was damaged.

6. A friend gave you an expensive vase for your birthday, but you didn't really like it.

ADVICE

_____ I guess I'd take it back to the store and exchange it for something else.

_____ I guess I'd write a letter of complaint to the manufacturer.

_____ Maybe I'd ask them to repair it.

_____ I think I'd make an appointment to see the instructor to talk about it.

_____ I'd probably wait until next month to see if they corrected their mistake.

_____ I'd write a letter to the city council and ask them to pay for the damage.

C Would you give the same advice or different advice for the problems above? Write **S** (same) or **D** (different). If you would give different advice, write what your advice would be.

Problem	Advice
1. ____	_____
2. ____	_____
3. ____	_____
4. ____	_____
5. ____	_____
6. ____	_____

5 *What would you have done in these situations? Use* **would have** *and* **wouldn't have.**

1. Diana had dinner in a restaurant and then realized she didn't have any money. She offered to wash the dishes.

   I wouldn't have washed the dishes. I would have called a friend to bring me money.

2. John doesn't smoke. He was on a bus when the woman next to him started smoking. He asked her to stop smoking.

   _____

   _____

3. Bill invited two friends to dinner on Friday, but they came on Thursday by mistake. He told them to come back the next day.

   _____

   _____

4. Bob's neighbors had their TV on very loud late at night. Bob called the police.

   _____

   _____

5. Ellen had a houseguest who was supposed to stay for three days, but she was still there three weeks later. Ellen gave her a bill for her room and board.

   _____

   _____

6. Susan accidentally broke a vase at a friend's house. She decided not to say anything about it.

   _____

   _____

6 *Write two things you should have done or shouldn't have done last week, last month, and last year.*

1. Last week: *I should have called my sister last week. . . .*

   _____

2. Last month: _____

   _____

3. Last year: _____

   _____

7 *Advice column*

A Complete each letter with the correct forms of the verbs in the box.

| ☐ borrow | ☑ marry | ☐ deny | ☐ return |
| ☐ disagree | ☐ save | ☐ enjoy | ☐ spend |

Dear Harriet,

I've never written to an advice column before, but I have a big problem. I'm going out with this really nice guy. He's very sweet to me, and I really want to _____ *marry* _____ him. In fact, we plan to have our wedding next summer. But he has a problem with money. He _____ money like crazy! Sometimes he _____ money from me, but he never _____ it. When I ask for my money back, he says he has none left. I want to _____ money because I want us to buy an apartment when we get married. However, if I tell him he has a problem with money, he says: "I _____ with you. You worry too much. You never want to go out and _____ yourself." As you can see, he just _____ his problem. What can I do?

J. M., Seattle

| ☐ accept | ☑ agree | ☐ find | ☐ admit | ☐ forget | ☐ refuse |

Dear J. M.,

You and your boyfriend must ____ *agree* ____ on how you spend your money *before* you get married. If you both _____ that there is a problem, you could probably _____ an answer. He should _____ your idea of saving some money. And you shouldn't always _____ to go out and have fun. Don't _____ that talking can really help. Good luck!

Harriet

B What would you advise J. M.? Write her a letter.

_____

_____

_____

_____

8 *To accept or to refuse?*

A Complete the conversation with *would* or *should* and the correct tense of the verbs given.

Judy: Guess what, Tina! The University of Auckland in New Zealand has

offered me a scholarship.

Tina: Great! When are you going?

Judy: That's just it. I may not go. What ___would___ you ___do___ (do) if

your boyfriend asked you not to go?

Tina: Well, I _____ (invite) him to come with me.

Judy: I've tried that. He said he won't go. And he might break up with me.

Tina: That's ridiculous! If I were you, I _____ (warn)

him not to try and control you. I missed a big opportunity once.

Judy: What happened?

Tina: I was offered a job in Thailand, but my husband disliked the idea, so we didn't

go. I _____ (take) the job. I've always regretted

my decision. In my situation, what _____ you _____ (do)?

Judy: Oh, I _____ (accept) the offer.

Tina: Well, there's the answer to your predicament. Accept your scholarship!

B What would you do if you were Judy? Why?

If I were Judy, . . . _____

_____

9 *What would you do if you found a magic lamp on a beach? Complete these sentences.*

1. I would *hide it and come back at sunset.* _____

2. I wouldn't _____

3. I could _____

4. I might _____

5. I might not _____

16 What's your excuse?

1 *People are making a lot of requests of James. Write the requests.*
Use **ask, tell,** *or* **say** *and reported speech.*

1. William: "James, take my phone calls."
2. Jenny: "Can you type some letters, James?"
3. Dave: "Could you make copies of these disks?"
4. Anita: "James, file these documents."
5. Linda: "Don't forget to add paper to the copier, James."
6. Ricky: "Fax this report to New York."
7. Chuck: "Make some coffee for me, James."
8. Katie: "Make five copies and don't give me any excuses."
9. Pete: "Could you give me a ride home?"
10. Olive: "Don't be late to work again."

1. *William asked James to take his phone calls.* _____
2. _____
3. _____
4. _____
5. _____
6. _____
7. _____
8. _____
9. _____
10. _____

2 Nouns and verbs

A Complete this chart.

Noun	Verb	Noun	Verb
acceptance	accept	_____	criticize
_____	apologize	_____	excuse
_____	complain	_____	invite
_____	compliment	_____	sympathize

B Complete these sentences. Use words from part A and the correct form of the verb where necessary.

1. This coffee tastes awful. I'll ___*complain*___ to the waiter about it.

2. I _____ an invitation to Terry and Anna's house for dinner.

3. I didn't want to go to Cindy's party, so I made up an _____ .

4. I was rude to my teacher. I must give him an _____ .

5. My English teacher _____ me on my homework. She said it was excellent. I was really surprised.

6. My parents _____ everything I do. I wish they weren't so negative.

7. I'm sorry you have the flu. I had it last week, so I really _____ with you.

8. I received an _____ to Janet's party. I can't wait to go.

3 Choose the correct verb. Use the past tense.

☐ express	☐ give	☑ make	☐ offer	☐ tell

1. I ___*made*___ a complaint to the police because our neighbors' party was too noisy.

2. Larry _____ me an apology. He asked me to forgive him because he forgot about the party.

3. I couldn't go to the meeting, so I _____ my regrets.

4. Wendy told me she was graduating from college, so I _____ her my congratulations.

5. Jill was very funny at the class party. As usual, she _____ lots of jokes.

4 *What a great excuse!*

A Match the invitations to the excuses. Underline the words and phrases that helped you.

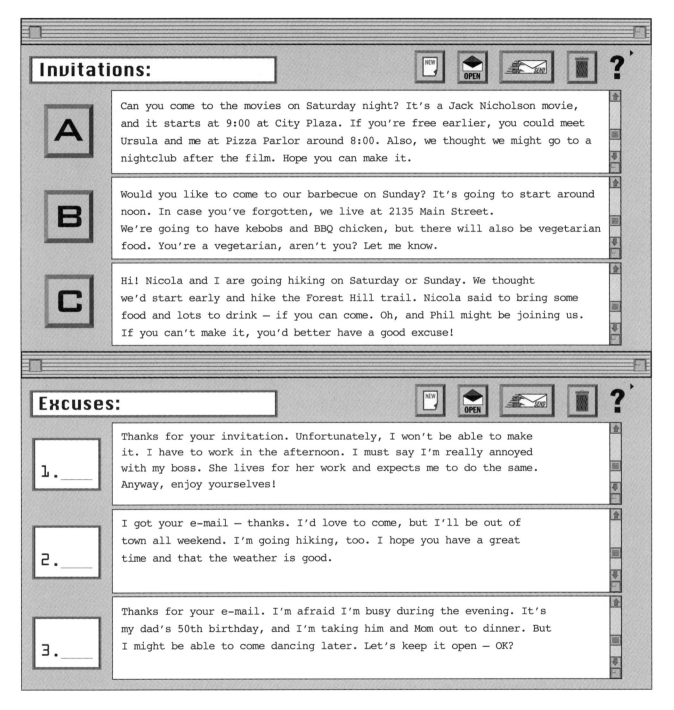

Invitations:

A Can you come to the movies on Saturday night? It's a Jack Nicholson movie, and it starts at 9:00 at City Plaza. If you're free earlier, you could meet Ursula and me at Pizza Parlor around 8:00. Also, we thought we might go to a nightclub after the film. Hope you can make it.

B Would you like to come to our barbecue on Sunday? It's going to start around noon. In case you've forgotten, we live at 2135 Main Street.
We're going to have kebobs and BBQ chicken, but there will also be vegetarian food. You're a vegetarian, aren't you? Let me know.

C Hi! Nicola and I are going hiking on Saturday or Sunday. We thought we'd start early and hike the Forest Hill trail. Nicola said to bring some food and lots to drink — if you can come. Oh, and Phil might be joining us. If you can't make it, you'd better have a good excuse!

Excuses:

1. ____ Thanks for your invitation. Unfortunately, I won't be able to make it. I have to work in the afternoon. I must say I'm really annoyed with my boss. She lives for her work and expects me to do the same. Anyway, enjoy yourselves!

2. ____ I got your e-mail — thanks. I'd love to come, but I'll be out of town all weekend. I'm going hiking, too. I hope you have a great time and that the weather is good.

3. ____ Thanks for your e-mail. I'm afraid I'm busy during the evening. It's my dad's 50th birthday, and I'm taking him and Mom out to dinner. But I might be able to come dancing later. Let's keep it open — OK?

B Read the excuses again. Who is going to do these things?
Write *1*, *2*, or *3*.

_____ be outdoors all weekend

_____ go out on the weekend

_____ work on the weekend

5 *Sorry, but . . . .*

A Look at these excuses that students gave to the teacher. Change them into reported speech. Use *say*.

1. John: "I'm getting my hair cut."
   John said he was getting his hair cut.

2. Maria: "My sister is having a baby."

   _____

3. Jim: "I may have some houseguests on Saturday."

   _____

4. Keiko and Kenji: "We're going camping this weekend."

   _____

5. Carlos: "I'm sorry, but I'll be busy on Saturday afternoon."

   _____

B Report these excuses that students gave to the teacher. Use *tell*.

1. Mary: "I signed up for a scuba diving class."
   Mary told her she had signed up for a scuba diving class.

2. Tom and Nancy: "We'll be moving to our new apartment that day."

   _____

3. Franco: "I watch the football game on TV every Sunday."

   _____

4. Juliet: "I've already made plans to do something else."

   _____

C Write excuses for two more students. Use your own ideas.

1. _____

2. _____

6 | *What did they say?*

A Match the reports of what people said in column A with the descriptions in column B.

A	B
1. Tina said she was really worried about Charlie. He seemed very depressed. __c__	**a.** giving an apology
2. William told me he was sorry he would be a little late to the party. _____	**b.** offering sympathy
3. Robert told me he couldn't come for dinner on Friday. He said he had to work late. _____	**c.** expressing a concern
4. Janice and Keith said they were really sorry we had the flu. They hoped we would feel better soon. _____	**d.** offering an invitation
5. Ben said he was going to ask Sarah to the party. _____	**e.** making an excuse

B Write each person's original words.

1. Tina: *"I'm really worried about Charlie. He seems very depressed."*

2. William: _____

_____

3. Robert: _____

_____

4. Janice and Keith: _____

_____

5. Ben: _____

_____

7 Choose the correct responses.

1. A: We're going to go horseback riding. Do you want to join us?

   B: _____

   - Sorry, I won't be able to.
   - What's up?

2. A: I'm really sorry. We'll be out of town this weekend.

   B: _____

   - I've made other plans.
   - No problem.

3. A: Meet us at 7:00. OK?

   B: _____

   - Oh, that's all right.
   - Sounds like fun.

4. A: I'm sorry. I won't be able to make it.

   B: _____

   - Well, never mind.
   - Great.

8 Yes or no?

A Which expressions would you use to accept an invitation? refuse an invitation? Check (✓) the correct answer.

	Accepting	Refusing		Accepting	Refusing
1. I'm really sorry.	☐	✓	5. I won't be able to make it.	☐	☐
2. Great.	☐	☐	6. I'm busy.	☐	☐
3. Sounds like fun.	☐	☐	7. Thanks a lot.	☐	☐
4. I've made other plans.	☐	☐	8. I'd love to.	☐	☐

B Use the expressions in part A to accept or refuse these invitations. Offer an excuse if you refuse.

1. A: Would you like to come to a photography class with me tomorrow?

   You: _____

2. A: Someone told me there was a good Australian movie at the Plaza. Do you want to see it with me this weekend?

   You: _____

3. A: A friend asked me to go shopping after class. Do you want to join us?

   You: _____